Bright Skies

Bright Skies

Selected Poems

by

Maja Trochimczyk

Moonrise Press, 2022

Copyright Information

Bright Skies. Selected Poems by Maja Trochimczyk is a book of poetry published by **Moonrise Press.** P.O. Box 4288, Los Angeles – Sunland, CA 91041-4288, www.moonrisepress.com.

© Copyright 2022 by Maja Trochimczyk.
All Rights Reserved 2022 by Moonrise Press
Cover design by Maja Trochimczyk, based on her photograph.

This book includes poems previously published in 2009 through 2022 in a variety of journals and books, as acknowledged with detailed prior publication credits on the following pages.

No part of this book may be reproduced or utilized in any form or by any means, electronic or mechanical, including photocopying and recording, or by any information storage and retrieval system, without permission in writing from the publisher.

Manufactured in the United States of America

The Library of Congress Publication Data:

Trochimczyk, Maja, 1957–
   [Poems. English.]
   Bright Skies. Selected Poems / Maja Trochimczyk, author

184 pages (x pp. prefatory matter, and 174 pp.); 6 in x 9 in. Written in English. With 162 photographs by Maja Trochimczyk, author's biographic note and 6 portraits.

ISBN 978-1-945938-49-8 (color paperback)

ISBN 978-1-945938-50-4 (color hardcover)

ISBN 978-1-945938-52-8 (eBook)

   I. Trochimczyk, Maja, 1957–Poetry. II. Title.

10 9 8 7 6 5 4 3 2 1

Table of Contents

Table of Contents ≈ v
Preface ≈ viii
Prior Publication Credits ≈ ix

Spring ~ Wiosna ≈ 3

1. A Springtime Revelation ≈ 4
2. Only in California ≈ 5
3. The Day of a Plum Tree ≈ 7
4. Outside my Window ≈ 9
5. Spring Cleaning ≈ 11
6. An Artichoke of a Poem ≈ 13
7. On Being Green in Vincent's Garden ≈ 15
8. Da Capo al Fine ≈ 17
9. A Ballad of a New Heart ≈ 19
10. An Invitation to the Dance ≈ 21
11. A Ballad of Angels ≈ 23
12. Practical Advice for a Frazzled Passer-by ≈ 25
13. Skylark's Lesson ≈ 27
14. Oh, The Art of Looking ≈ 29
15. On Being a Bird ≈ 31
16. the doves of love ≈ 32
17. A Mystery Solved ≈ 33
18. Double Delight ≈ 35
19. Diamond Days in Crystal Gardens ≈ 36
20. This Afternoon ≈ 39
21. From Minium Chronicles ≈ 40
22. The Golden Hour ≈ 42

Summer ~ Lato ≈ 43

1. June in Gold and Blue ≈ 44
2. The Song of the Summer ≈ 46
3. A Tale of a Hare ≈ 48
4. A Drink of Water ≈ 50
5. Mason Bees ≈ 51

6. The Golden Time of Honey ≈ 53
7. Dreaming Bees ≈ 55
8. A Pear in a Tree ≈ 56
9. A Day Trip to Venice, California ≈ 57
10. Carving Sand ≈ 59
11. A Champagne Sunday ≈ 61
12. Aquamarine ≈ 63
13. The Ocean of Jade ≈ 65
14. The 23rd of July ≈ 67
15. *Tatarak* ≈ 69
16. Flying Kites ≈ 71
17. "Let me go!" ≈ 73
18. Soap Bubbles ≈ 74
19. High Noon ≈ 75
20. *Matka Boska Zielna* ≈ 76
21. In Morning Light ≈ 78

Babie Lato ≈ 81

1. On Thursday Afternoon ≈ 82
2. Sapphire ≈ 84
3. Amber ≈ 85
4. A Revelation after *Il Paradiso* ≈ 86
5. Up, Up, Up ≈ 88
6. From Yesterday's Dream ≈ 89
7. Sunfire Foxes ≈ 91
8. Sweet Nothings ≈ 92
9. The Year of Crystal Fire ≈ 94
10. Just to Make It Clear ≈ 96
11. A Chromosome Ballad ≈ 97
12. Twin Flame Promise ≈ 98
13. Diamonds ≈ 100

Autumn ~ Jesien ≈ 101

1. On Cosmic Breath ≈ 102
2. Landscapes: A Guidebook ≈ 103
3. A Cosmic Rainbow ≈ 106
4. Today – For Us ≈ 110

5. I Give You the World ≈ 112
6. A Golden Poem for a Girl of Gold ≈ 122
7. Gold Wishes ≈ 124
8. Juniper ≈ 127
9. The Fierce Explorer ≈ 128
10. The Aril ≈ 130
11. Fall Yucca ≈ 132
12. This Evening ≈ 135
13. Diamond Rain ≈ 136

Winter ~ Zima ≈ 139

Coda ~ Recipes for Poems ≈ 168

Spring – *Mazurkas* ≈ 168
Summer – Pickled Pears and Plums ≈ 169
Babie Lato – *Szarlotka* ≈ 170
Autumn – *Bigos* and Salads ≈ 171
Winter – *Barszcz, Kompot* and *Kutia* ≈ 172

About the Author ≈ 173

Preface

This collection of poems is inspired by the births of my two granddaughters, Aurelia, born on 12 September 2021 and Juniper, born on 16 September 2021. I planned to write a book of poems for each girl, just as I did for my grandson, Adam, born on 16 September 2016. The poetry book dedicated to him, entitled *I Give You the World*, contains one long poem describing things that I love and cherish in this life, illustrated with photos of my family, travels, and gardens. An abridged version without family pictures appeared on my blog; this version is further shortened here. The purpose of the book for Adam was to introduce the Polish-born boy to his American & Canadian family and their lives. He now lives in the U.S. and is able to share these delights in-person.

Since Adam got "the whole world" as his birthday present, what can I give to his five-years-younger sister, Aurelia, and his cousin, Juniper? I found 85 poems and over 160 photographs that I decided to share with them, in a book to be read when they grow up. This is not a children's book. With gratitude, I described delights that I found in my garden and home, during walks, adventures, and travels. I wrote about inspirational moments and discoveries, summarizing my life's wisdom at 64. This volume of "positive poetry" contains verse originally written in 2009 -2022 and is a companion volume to *Into Light: Poems and Incantations* (2016). It is a necklace of love and blessings; each bead – a poem.

I hope that the readers attracted to the themes of seeking light and enjoying life in the garden will find here something to enjoy, something to think about, and something to do in their own lives. After all, we live in the Garden of Eden and can make this Earth a Paradise, if we only want to. Enjoy!

Maja Trochimczyk
Los Angeles, 1 June 2022

Prior Publication Credits

Most of poems included here have been posted on my *Poetry Laurels* blog and included in anthologies or journals in somewhat different versions.

"Amber," "This Afternoon," "A Ballad of New Heart," "A Day Trip to Venice," "Diamonds," "High Noon," "Gifts," "Imagine – A Poem of Light," "Just to Make it Clear," "Landscapes: A Guidebook," "Sunfire Foxes," "Your Rainbow," "Sapphire," " "Sweet Nothings," "Twin Flame Promise," in *Rose Always - A Love Story* (Moonrise Press, 2020).

"Aquamarine," *California Quarterly,* 46: 4, Winter 2020.

"Arbor Cosmica" *California Quarterly,* 44: 1, Spring 2018.

"From Minium Chronicles" and "Practical Advice for a Frazzled Passer- by," *California Quarterly,* 48: 1, Spring 2022.

"Crystal Light of Crystal Mornings," *When The Virus Came Calling: COVID19 Strikes America,* ed. Thelma T. Reyna, September 2020.

"De Capo Al Fine," *Quill & Parchment,* vol. 249, March 2022.

"A Champagne Sunday," *Blue and the Blues*, ed. Carole Boyce, 2021.

"A Declaration," and a different version of "Today," *Into Light. Poems & Incantations* (Moonrise Press, 2016).

"The Golden Time of Honey," *Quill & Parchment,* vol. 253, July 2022.

"I Give You the World," excerpts from a book of the same title, (Moonrise Press, 2016, limited edition).

"Imagine – A Poem of Light," "Sapphire," "June in Gold and Blue" in *We Are Here: Village Poets Anthology* (Moonrise Press, 2020).

"In Morning Light," *Grateful Conversations* (Moonrise Press, 2018),

"An Invitation to the Dance," *Altadena Poetry Review*, April 2016.

"A Jewel Box Sunrise," *San Gabriel Valley Poetry Quarterly* 52, winter 2011, reprinted in *From Benicia with Love*, ed. Don Peery, 2013.

"Matka Boska Zielna," *Quill & Parchment,* vol. 251, May 2022.

"A Mystery Solved," "On Being a Bird," "A Drink of Water," "Song of the Summer" in *Zwierzenia Zwierza* (Bezkres, 2020).

"Oh, the Art of Looking," *California Quarterly* 44: 4, Winter 2018,

"Only in California," *The Voice of the Village,* 2: 7, May 2011.

"On Being Green in Vincent's Garden," *Spectrum,* vol. 18, Spring 2019.

"A Pear in a Tree," *The Voice of the Villagex,* 3: 8, August 2012.

"A Revelation After *Il Paradiso*," *Angel City Review,* No. 3, 2016.

"Rules for Happy Holy Days," *The Voice of the Village*, 3: 12, 2012.

"Skylark's Lesson," *Lummox Poetry Journal,* vol. 8, 2019.

""Winter Solstice," *Spectrum,* vol. 17, December 2018.

Bright Skies

~ for my children

and their children

when they grow up

SPRING ~ WIOSNA

A Springtime Revelation

I love my mountains
blue and spring green, still
under clear azure expanse.
Their velvet pleats pile up
in layers above the valley rocks,
pathways in empty riverbed.

This is the Earth — naked,
free of trees and houses, of rush
and pavement and cars on hot asphalt
in L.A. summers — this is pure repose
— serenely breathing, slowly, deeply
in the cycle of centuries, eons.

I love my mountains —
the bluish shadows on distant slopes
manzanita and sage scattered

close-by. The hills open like curtains
into infinity to let me in—beyond the next
peak, the next canyon, into new worlds
that thrive in golden sunlight, expand under
the cool glow of spiraling galaxies before dawn.

I'm here, I found my life waiting for me
under the indigo cupola outlined
with deep purple at the ridges—here
crickets measure the night as they sing
"we are here   here here here   here here"
while birds sleep, hidden among branches.

Only distant waves of truck noise
from the freeway remind me that
this paradise of mine, this fluid, living
folding and unfolding is my L.A. home
hidden in a strange metropolis,
my own La La Land of bare mountains,
and the brightest of sunlit gardens.

Only in California

The desert is rich with the noise
of our ghost river, suddenly filled
with mocha cappuccino, a swirl
of white frothy foam on the surface.

Chuparosa and sunrose blossom.
The moving white spot of a rabbit's tail
disappears between sticky snapdragons,
goldenrod, and pearly everlasting.

The last red leaves tremble on the tips
of tree branches. The liquid amber
is bare; the gingko, no longer golden—
a skeleton waiting for summer.

One by one, scarlet star-shapes fall
onto the green carpet of new grass.
The shoots of narcissus and hyacinth
peek through the weight of dead foliage.

Puffy pink clouds surround the disc
of the moon, shining on the smooth
turquoise. Seasons melt in a day.

The sun smiles at the audacity
of this preposterous, beyond belief,
one and only, California spring.

The Day of a Plum Tree

Like a pink anemone
at the bottom of the sea
stamens dance in slow motion

Plum flowers open and stretch
towards the sun — the sun — the sun

They drink dew and juices of the earth
flowing up roots, trunk, branches

Their petals, like layers of crinoline skirts,
fold and unfold, re-arranging themselves
around dark plum-hued heart of hearts

Dancing stamens wait for the bees
to make honey and fruit out of
their passing beauty

Soon,
        breeze will rise
among branches —
        pink blizzard
of swirling petals   will waltz
        through the air
to the ground   to the roots
      into oblivion

    The flowering
        of the plum tree
    once again

Outside my Window

A round spot of gold light appears
on the smooth slope of California hills
green in the spring, shadowed by rainclouds.

> Suddenly, an epiphany of light
> blossoms among thickening shadows,
> dusk approaching soon, much too soon.

The shining circle stretches into an arrow,
points west, along the ridge. The arrow of light,
my arrow, tells me to go, do, act, lead and follow.
Be the light, bring the light. Enlighten.

> Before I can even reach for pen and paper
> to write down this command, this call to action,
> it is gone. All is shadow now. Murky darkness.

Yet the memory of the cloud epiphany lingers,
etched onto my retina. This spot of light,
this arrow will always be with me—

Each morning, I will turn the circle of contemplation
into the arrow of action, the dawn star
into a comet, inexorably reaching its end.

> Is it not the story of my life?
> This spot of light on a mountain meadow
> after one winter storm, before another?

I catch it, hold it, and keep it safe
among my treasures. Things not to be
discarded. Unforgettable thoughts.

> Another pearl for my precious necklace
> woven from brilliant moments—
> jewels of a well-lived life.

Spring Cleaning

This morning I declawed the cactus,
cut the spikes from the tips of agave leaves
so they do not scratch children looking for
chocolate eggs on Easter.

I cleaned out the pantry, sorted out
one bookshelf and my past
carefully discarding useless fears
and fading disappointments.

I filled the crystal bird dish
with water for finches, filled my heart
with affection and delight.

I arranged lilacs, and daffodils
into fragrant bouquets, green with
camellia leaves and palm fronds left over
from singing Hosanna in the church.

I arranged my thoughts
into a singular clarity of purpose.
Tranquil, like the Pacific at sunset,
with tenderness of immense strength.

Now, I only have to breathe in
hot noon light, to set old pain,
anger and resentment on fire,

expel the ashes in a shower of sparks
with diamond rays so brilliant,
they make me into a supernova
a revelation, cosmic, bright —

An Artichoke of a Poem

Writing poetry is like growing
artichokes, from a seed of invention,
the code for the unknown, sprouts
an immense plant, with spreading
silvery-green fronds of tender beauty—
poem after poem you spin out and admire,
so proud of your way with words,
constructing verbal edifices
with arduous labor.

The heart comes at the end—
a flower bud no larger than your palm
that does not even open before you pick it
to steam and taste bits of elegance
and sophistication.

High above your silver tower of gigantic
soft and spiky leaves—a paradox of a plant,

really, its purpose beyond comprehension —
grows just one artichoke, a golden bud
of a poem where each word is in its place,
each insight so accurate and keen,
it pierces the reader's mind
with knowing.

You discard abundant, decorative
leaves for compost, to nourish next year's crop —
just one gourmet treat, an artichoke of a poem,
blooming from so many ornamental words
you string together day after day, until
the mystery
     reveals itself
          to surprise you
               with its inevitable
                    simple grace —

On Being Green in Vincent's Garden

> ~ After Vincent Van Gogh, "The Poet's Garden" (1888)
> at the Art Institute of Chicago

A white rose faints on a cement sidewalk.
Crisp clear azure sky encloses the city in a cupola.
Art vibrates on the walls of the Art Institute
guarded by green-patinaed copper lions
in garish Christmas wreaths. Van Gogh
waits for me. Frowning, uncertain.

Yes, I love your iridescent greens,
celadons, aquas, emeralds, jades.
The vibrant grass, uncut new meadow
and the explosion of bushes and trees,
vibrating with the full force of life.

Leaf opens after leaf — after leaf —
exploding with cosmic energy
alive — so alive — so alive — so alive
so real, emerging from canvas
coming into becoming — stretching —
growing — being — breathing — living —

Even the sky vibrates in hues of green
and yellow, turquoise, and aqua.
Each plant, tree, bush — marked with
a thick layer of paint, intense brushstrokes.
I understand now. Vincent was one
of us, the seeing ones. Awake.
He could not tell us any louder
than in this saturated greenest paint.

> *Open your eyes. We are all here.*
> *The world is ours to love, to see.*

Da Capo Al Fine

dark green
       light green
              moss green
                     sage green

The world is verdant with life
spring foliage unfurls from wine-red
buds, luxuriating in sunlight.

Mockingbirds' melodious argument
resonates through the garden—
"This is my, my, my tree!""
"Oh, no! Oh, no! Oh, no!"

Air fills with the intense scent
of orange blossoms and the warm gold
to mauve, to vermilion glow of April roses

dark green
    light green
        moss green
            sage green

The silvery hue of sweet alyssum
reminds me of sea foam on aqua waves
of the Pacific I can only admire on my laptop
until the "stay at home" orders are lifted
and beaches are as full of human life
as vibrant as my rainbow-green garden
in these wartimes of a strange plague.

dark green
    light green
        moss green
            sage green

Da Capo Al Fine

A Ballad of a New Heart

Once I found a rock heart, my heart of hard rock.
I took it to carry with me.

Along muddy shores of the river of time
that flows down in the ravine.

I carry my rock as I walk up the hill
of a thousand stones, all so cold.

The rock now softens and moves in my hands,
it melts into heart of pure gold.

I carry my gold heart up the mountain, up high,
I carry, I carry its weight.

With each step it's heavier, its surface so hard
careful, it might slip out of my hands.

I know how the river races down, full of mud
I'm lucky I turned to go up.

This weight is for me to carry alone.
It is my heart of rock, my own task.

It starts feeling alive, in the warmth of my hands
I thought it was only a rock.

I cradle it safely in my two folded arms
as I bring it up high, to the top.

The sky is clear, blue. Winter storms have all passed.
I look at smooth river below.

I thought it was muddy, full of dirt as it rushed
but it sparkles with rainbows aglow.

It's my river that flows, my heart changed to flesh
I discovered my treasure of old.

You will, too, find your heart, change rock into gold
to cherish, to love, and to hold.

An Invitation to the Dance

And the angels are dancing.
Did you say dancing? Yes, dancing. Making somersaults
and jumping two hundred yards in the air.
*Air? Are they here? I thought they lived in infinity,
or eternity, or the great beyond, or whatchamacallit.*

No. Here. They are laughing their heads off. Giggling,
smiling, smirking, guffawing. Laughing.
What's so funny? Nic. Nada. Naught. It is just that they are
so happy. So incredibly, exorbitantly, blissfully happy.
Why? Oh, because of that quirky thing
from the country song.

What thing? Don't you know? Have you not heard
that love conquers all? That love triumphs
over lies, fear, anger, shame and despair?

That it is? Love is. True love. Our love…
It blossoms in us, through us.
It opens its petals. The world is more tranquil,
serene in the luminescence of our love.
New stars are born. Cherries are sweeter when we
are together, immersed in this love. When we
find it. Return to it. Share it. Cherish it. When we
are not giving up. No matter what. No matter how hard.
No matter how late. It is quite simple, so simple.
Impossible? Yet, it is here to stay.

So, what about these angels, then?
Oh, yes. Would you like to go dancing with angels?
Boogie-woogie, waltz, tango, or salsa?

A Ballad of Angels

If I were an angel,
I'd know how not to cry.
Everything would be perfect
In my gold-winged life.

If I were an angel,
White star within my heart,
My path, the space around me
Would sparkle in the night.

If I were an angel,
You would not hear me lie.
Truth is so simple, always
It teaches us to fly.

Oh, wait! I am an angel
Wrapped in a rainbow glow.
I dance like crimson sunbird
In clear skies high above.

I am God's Light servant.
I speak, I walk in truth.
Dazzling, resplendent quetzal
turns dark to dawn to noon.

Angels are all connected
To serve the greatest good
So, every living creature
Is happy as they should.

We too, can be angelic,
Filled with the divine grace
If we throw off our burdens
Of guilt, of shame, of vice.

Our path is clear and narrow
Don't seek forbidden fruit.
Follow the guidance given
Step onwards, foot by foot.

We'll reach our destination
Our wings grown wide and bright.
Hearts soft, like dove's feathers
We'll dance high up, in the light.

Practical Advice for a Frazzled Passer-by

When you reach the nadir of darkness —
shine.

When a stranger pushes you on a sidewalk
say, "Sunshine, smile" — and shine again.
Think of the hand of a newborn resting in your palm,
five fingers smaller than the smallest of yours —
a miracle coming into being.

Glow
with the tender infinity
of diamond light flowing out of your heart —
your best kept secret — you are the sun, the ascending spiral
of timeless presence — embodied wisdom — infinite charm —
the trinity of loving-kindness — the living crystal

constantly reborn, outflowing from the reservoir
of divine grace you did not know you were — are —
dazzling brightness — sparkling, twirling
in an aetheric waltz of nascent cosmos
that comes into being in you —
through you —
with you —

Say YES

so it comes — comes — comes —

again —

Skylark's Lesson

Don't strive. Don't fight.
Don't go beyond yourself, tensely stretching
reaching, grasping, in an effort
to bend reality to your own will
"I want, I want, I want..."

Listen. Leave this. Relax into Love
surrounding you like the smooth surface
of a mountain lake, rosy at dawn,
reflecting clearly the splendor
of crystalline peaks, glistening
with new snow, in tranquil stillness.

Be glad, so glad. Be calm, so calm. Content.
Breathe deeply. Fill your whole being
with happiness found among white daisies,
fragrant clover and golden dandelions
on a spring meadow, under the bell

of a sky, ringing with pure tones
of a lone skylark that sings away,
up in the azure, among puffy white clouds
The sky is mirrored in the softness
of cornflowers and bluebells.

Be still, so still, like a pine forest
 at noon, hot with the fullness of summer
treetops barely stirring in the light breeze
whispering to each other, to you
to the birds, weary with sleep after
their extravaganza of the dawn chorus.

The Sun is up. The Sun is up.
The Sun is everywhere. The Sun
caresses our crowns and we
grow – grow – – grow – – –
from deep waters of the Earth
into Sunlight.

Breathe deeply, slowly, deeply.
IN – the tension constricting your heart
with worries of today, yesterday, tomorrow.
OUT – the openness of Love, of loving all,
seeing all, touching all, being all,
flowing freely, brilliantly in waves
of liquid light – within you, around you,
over you – here, now, always, now –

Relax into Love. Be still, so still.
Be glad, so glad, be happy.
Blossom like the Earth's gentle smile,
like the *khorovod* of trees, birds' servants
sustaining all among their leaves and branches.

Is there anything you want to know?
The answer is here already,
waiting for you in the center
of your open heart.

Oh, the Art of Looking

Look ahead—
wave and wave and wave

dance in the moonlight
a silver path across the ocean
shimmering horizon
stark intensity
of the Pacific

Look up—
the Milky Way
What do you see?
The spine of the world?
Buttons made of stars?
Indigo cupola with diamonds?

wave after wave after wave

Look inside—
deep into my eyes
electric currents flow
in an arc of brightness
connecting us into One
the Oneness we forgot

Now, we are alive, we are One—
the clear azure
of windswept sky—
the ruby wine
beneath roots
of the earth

Look around—
wake up and see,

truly see where you are —
enveloped in a blanket
of time, carried
from now to now —

from wave to wave to wave

from Earth into Earth into One

On Being a Bird

A flock of birds alights in my garden.
Smaller than sparrows, they chase each other
from tree to tree, branch to branch—chattering
incessantly in their ultraviolent voices. My ears fill
with a sonic kaleidoscope, at limits of the audible range.

They will rest and fly away, satiated
with shreds of rose petals, bits of a ripening peach
shared with red house finches that visit at noon.
They grow quiet at the cawing of a crow or meowing
of a stray predator cat that passes through
on its errands, pretending to be kind.

Would I be happy as a bird?
I see wings in flight. Lightness. Music.
I forget hidden dangers lurking in the sky,
among dense, overgrown branches. I forget
rains and the plight of modern subdivisions
without trees— built by those who love only
one hue of green and it is not of plants.

Not of my Planetary Church of Plants and Birds,
I founded eight years ago in my garden, alone with
the Sun and Air and Earth and Water—I took the oath
of a caretaker—no toxins, no traps, just green,
verdant green, greening. This is our home to share,
our vibrant garden of daily nourishment and joy.

the doves of love
line up in my sky
for a new song

A Mystery Solved

"Look, a goldfinch is eating a yellow rose. Oh, wait,
it is an Oriole." Quite fittingly named. The rose is Oregold.
Oro, d'or, aurum — the most precious treasure, so vivid,
so alive. It is all about flashy feathers in sunny hues
contrasting with black wings, head, tail. Golden
blossoms flourish among vibrant, green leaves.
The Oriole wife, in camouflage, opts for a mundane
meal, picking ants and roly-polies off the lawn.
Striped with gray, she is used to living in his shade.

Look, another Oriole nibbles on a silver-red, two-tone
rose of love, by the pomegranate. What a scene!
Dazzling colors outlined against white walls of an old
shed at the end of a pathway lined with river rocks.
Pity, I cannot take a picture. I drowned my cell phone
in a mountain stream on Sunday. An accident waiting
to happen for 13 years, since I fell down a flight of stairs

and did not break my arms in five places, as doctors
thought, X-raying me to smithereens. Instead, I lost grip
in my fingers. I drop things when I do not pay attention.

"Take a picture with your eyes, Mom." My daughter
used to say. Enamored with a brand—new camera, I'd stop
at every blooming rose, slowing down the progress
of a family walk years ago. My kids have left. I wade
in streams alone. I have all the time in the world to explore
the geometry of petals, from every angle documenting
for posterity the ephemeral gold-and-scarlet rainbow.

I've wondered why my fully open roses have
such shredded edges, why they lose perfection quickly.
I see it today. I take a picture with my eyes, as I sip amber
tea from a golden-white porcelain teacup and admire an oriole
eating my Oregold rose for a fancy, fragrant breakfast.

Double Delight

Gentle as dawn, clearing
the sky of midnight nightmares
my April rose smiles to herself
rearranging the blush and pink crinoline
of petals folded into a heart—
her secret within
She tells me to laugh
and laugh again, overflowing
with childish joy, champaign bubbling
in a glass—while the air around me
is heavy with cries of panic, anguish, hate.
"What of the news?" you say,
*"Who lived, who died, who suffered?"
My April rose smiles to herself.
I'm silent, exploring the inner landscapes
that only music knows—the infinity
of cellos, violins, and the lover's gaze
locked in the key of brightness.

Diamond Days in Crystal Gardens

Once I was a Princess of Shining Flame
a Rose in the Palace of Fire
searching for my Knight of Lightning,
my Prince of the Sun Chariot.

I looked and looked, in one country, the next.
I crossed the ocean, lured by the siren call
of the unknown, enchanted by its blissful promise.

I will not tell you what I found and discarded,
time and time again — like Doc in the diamond mine
throwing away jewels of dark hues, listening
for flaws in their voices. I left behind what was no longer
needed, even pity that I wished for these things at all.

Now, I'm the Queen of the Throne of Violet Flame,
the Empress of Contentment. I find untold treasures

in my garden, sheltered by seven hills and dales,
protected by blue agave and the thorns of my roses.
Emerald tree leaves glow under sapphire cupola.
Diamond dew drops cover my lawn
with a fortune of good wishes.

From dawn to dusk, hummingbirds, finches
and doves fill the air with the flutter of wings,
fluted arabesques of their calls. They rest at noon
for a moment of awe at the Majesty, the Sun.

I rest here, too, caressed by the breeze,
scented by orange blossoms, mint, and jasmine.
I drink from the clear streams of living waters.

I pick wildflowers from sun-drenched meadows—
red poppies, sun-like daisies, blue stars of cornflowers
and forget-me-nots, all wrapped in green lace of forest fern.

I give away rich bouquets of velvet roses—
burgundy, Oregold and alba, with shades of
mauve, peach, and vermillion.

Would you like a bouquet like that?

I am the Empress of Contentment. My realm stretches
as far as I can see—to the horizon of Pacific Ocean,
shimmering in the summer heat, bringing homage
of wave after wave to my sandy toes.

I find seashells, with endless melodies within,
reaching to the most distant galaxies
of midnight heavens.

I glow brighter than the brightest star.
I'm a rainbow of infinite radiance.
All made of Love, I'm the fountain of Light,
cresting wave in the Cosmic Ocean.

This Afternoon

> *You are the music while the music lasts.*
> ~ T.S. Eliot, *Little Gidding*

The woodpecker measures time by the thickness
of tree trunks. Birds make nests, hidden from
hawks, safe from scrub jays. We wake in sunlight,
with twirling patterns still under our closed eyelids.

We listen to high-pitched calls of hummingbirds,
the random flutter of wings. We breathe in spring air
with smoothly flowing melodies of birdsong,
the sweetest of nectars. Waves crash on distant shores
of the Pacific. Stars appear dimly above the horizon,
that glows with the bronzed orange of departing Sun.

We live on the planet of children's laughter.
We watch refractions of light in my sapphire ring,
on diamond dew drops that cling to blades of grass,
half-opened roses. We live on Earth of abundance
and beauty. We live on Earth of plenitude and calm.

There are no sorrows here, no worries.
No before, nor after. No plans. We take deep
breaths, count to eight, inhaling smiles to the tips
of our fingers, into our toes. I laugh. You laugh.
Crystalline peals echo through the Universe —
from galaxy to galaxy, star to star.

We grow and grow — infinite, gentler, wiser —
we understand all, embrace all, know all.
Perfection. Presence. Light.

From Minium Chronicles

~ for my children

A tall glass of water and three oranges,
A tall glass of water and three oranges,
three blood oranges from a tree I planted
ten years ago, in my Sunland garden.

A tall glass of water... Am I a lump of clay
that's returning to Earth? Ashes to ashes?
The journey's done, nothing remains?

Am I a star of unsung brilliance hidden in a fragile body —
learning, collecting wisdom of limitation, before
my triumphant return to the glory of timeless Now?

Am I saved? Redeemed? Do I need a Savior?
Am I my own savior, perhaps? What is true?
What is real? Ashes to ashes, or light into Light?

A tall glass of water and three blood oranges
for breakfast. I'm grateful for the knowledge
they impart. What I am. What I'm made of.

The abundance of rain and sweetness of sunlight
fills the fruit with fragrant, rosy juice, under
 the soft, pliable rind — so lovely inside and outside.

A fruit of the earth, air, water, fire nourishes me
with elements. The fruit I made now fills me
with morning happiness in the rain.

Soothing patter of raindrops on the patio roof
assures me that questions do not matter,
answers do not matter either.

It is the NOW of breathing, of tasting that
slightly tart, refreshing orange I grew, a jewel
I add to the beads of memories I keep.

The Golden Hour

The mockingbird leads a chorus
of orioles, black phoebes, bluebirds,
finches, juncos, and ruby crowned kinglets.

The buzzing you hear is not dangerous,
these are Anna's hummingbird's wings.

Birds crowd around the fountain,
water droplets scatter on sandy path.

The afternoon sighs with relief.
All is well and all shall be well
in our garden at four o'clock.

SUMMER ~ LATO

June in Gold and Blue

> *"It was June and the world smelled like roses. The sunshine was like powdered gold over the grassy hillside."*
> *~ Maud Hart Lovelace*

Hidden among stiff, broad, dark-green leaves, as if from
an exotic isle, ripe bunches of loquat glow in afternoon sunrays
like "powdered gold" scattered on the slopes across the valley.

I am content to share a loquat, juice dripping down
my chin, with a woodpecker that cut a groove in one side,
tasting its tart sweetness. With a shrill call, the bird flies
along a sine wave — rising, falling — too heavy for its wings.

I thought it was a parrot, one of Pasadena invaders,
relentlessly chased away by my resident finches and doves.
I am relieved to see a scarlet spot on its head,
black-and-white striped wings peeking beneath tree branches.

"Hello, my dear. Welcome to my June Paradise. Please enjoy
the fruit on the top. I cannot climb so high. Let's share these
life-giving delights." The bird will not stay long. Its departure
will leave a strange gash of absence, stretching shadows in its wake.

Just like that dolphin, ten years ago, that joined our boat trip to
Catalina, jumping above waves with such glee, we laughed aloud.
The dolphin laughed too, playfully teasing us with his ephemeral
dance, contours outlined against the blue expanse of water and air.

Just like the striking, gold-furred grizzly bear, a mountain
of primeval power, curling to sleep on my lawn. *Misiek.*
My Protector. I'd swear I saw him once, at sunset. He came
to my Oasis to rest, dream lucid dreams about me—

as I eat luscious loquats straight off the tree, listen
to euphonious birdsong, gaze at the azure clarity
of endless sky. Serene, I am here, where I belong.
The taste of summer fruit. One June after another.

The Song of the Summer

The house finches are back! The four little ones disappeared
on Friday. Their crowded nest under the porch roof
was full of wide-open yellow beaks crying out for breakfast.
Now, blades of grass are scattered on my front steps.
The nest is empty. They learned how to fly.

I was happy yet sad, a bittersweet moment.
My home was their home. They grew up undisturbed
on my porch, in the nest tucked on top of a white
wooden beam. Gone to their new adventures
like my children to Boston, Tucson, San Diego.

Look, my finches are back! They returned to the only
home they knew to practice flight from rooftop to rooftop,
from garage to the end of my driveway, the Japanese pine
that all birds love to perch on, its branches stretching
like fingers to the sky — an open palm of a tree.

Listen, my finches are back! They study their song
at six in the morning. It is a simple, repetitive phrase
spiraling down through fluted eddies of pure music,
measuring the hours of summer. The song never
changes, I used to think it boring—a step up from
the monotone chirping of sparrows, and yet—

My finches are back! And they are learning to sing.
Note by note, motif by motif, they try out brief snatches
of their Dad's tune and fail, and fail, and fail again.
I did not know it's so hard. The three notes on the top
ti-ti-ti—are easy—but, as the descending swirls begin,
at a top speed, like droplets in a mountain stream rushing down,
sparkling in sunlight—the birds stop, confused.

"Let me show you, how it's done!" Patient parent sings
again and again. Young birds repeat the patterns in shy,
quiet voices, growing louder, more confident, true—
until they, too, sing their hearts out in joy.

See? The finches are back!

A Tale of a Hare

A rabbit moved into my garden.
A wild hare, rather — sandy gray
with a rusty spot on the back of the neck,
darker tips of pinkish ears and a white furball
of a tail, just like in a cartoon.

My rabbit looks at me askew with a curious,
black, round eye and slowly hops away
to nibble on blades of grass or rest in the middle
of my driveway — really, he thinks he owns this street.

He's not afraid, just puzzled by my presence
in this paradise of greenery and shade he found
for himself when he left the chapparal to explore.

It is safe here. He has a bodyguard, Attila,
an Australian Shepherd that walks around stately

protecting the neighborhood with a serious air
of a victor in countless skirmishes with coyotes.

My lovely, brave hare is safe with me, under
the watchful eyes of fierce Attila. He must have heard
of the cornucopia of my wild yard from passing birds
flocking here daily to rest and keep insects in check.

His presence tames my heart—a gift from Gaia
for these hard times of the plague of hatred
and distress. I wonder about the instinct of trust
in my non-toxic overgrown refuge of co-existence.
I'm so glad to share my plants with a wild hare.

A Drink of Water

The forest is on fire. A racoon knows how
to stay alive. he has moved into my garage.
He ate a box of candles I kept for emergencies
on the counter, licked clean a plastic plate
with a melted one, stuck away in a corner.

I see muddy footprints on the washing machine.
He walked across to get a drink of water at the sink,
left the faucet slightly open, with water dripping.
I have to teach him how to close it fully,
not waste the precious white gold in the desert.

My next-door neighbor heard the noise, came over
to look one night, banging on the garbage bins
in my driveway. I don't want my resident racoon
to be shot with the black, dead-looking gun—a pistol
from my neighbor's shelf, kept, just in case, by the door.

My racoon has moved back into my garage. It was his
country before I came from Canada in the 90ties,
before the house was built in 1948, before an artificial
lake flooded the plane of an ancient riverbed in 1910,
before an orange grove was planted in the 1880s.

Two world wars, a Cold War, and a War on Terror later,
a racoon, my racoon has moved back into my garage.
I have to teach it how to fully close the faucet, so it stops
dripping, wasting the precious white gold of water
in the desert—water in my home—water in his—water—

Mason Bees

I share my roses with the mason bees —
Iceberg leaves they like the best, cutting
circles and ellipses from the edge, inwards.

Iceberg roses, not iceberg lettuce, mind you,
that's far too crunchy to make soft beds, wrapping
bee babies in green, white, or pink silkiness,

smooth and pliable like we ought to be, smiling
under the merciless gale of time, raging river
flowing backwards, always backwards.

I used to get angry looking at my mutilated roses —
white blossoms, a defense against evil guarding my
front door like bee soldiers in the hive

ready to sacrifice themselves—just one sting
and the miniature fuzzy warrior's gone—having
lived just to protect and serve us, the worker bees,

buzzing around our lives, cutting circles and
ellipses in white roses. Bees and humans, we are
all children of the Queen Bee, Gaia, our Mother.

We make honey of our kindness, virtues, character
wisdom, self-reliance. Attentive, focused on the next
perfect circle, semicircle, or ellipsis—we breathe deeply,

delight in drinking nectar, carrying pollen of emotions,
sights, impressions—flying back home to make the sweetest
gold, translucent honey of our poems, of our dreams.

The Golden Time of Honey

*~ for Grandma Nina Trochimczyk and
bees in her linden tree in Bielewicze*

My grandma had a huge linden tree to shade her yard
growing right in the middle, dividing it in half, where
the orchard and garden ended and where the farm machines
were parked by the barn, full of hay. My uncle made a small
wooden bench to sit under that ancient tree. At least 300 years
old, it was just a shade tree until it came alive each July —
so loud, full of bees, busy, buzzing. Linden flowers are small,
abundant, whitish yellow. The linden honey is light in hue,
like clover, with a different, delicate scent. What a pleasure
to rest in the shade and listen to the bees making honey.

*golden summer
under the linden tree
full of honeybees*

The buckwheat honey is more aromatic, darker, like Baltic amber. Once, when I was strolling through the buckwheat fields with my brother, we walked by a beekeeper's orchard guarded by a tall fence. A swarm of bees escaped with their new queen. Alas, they found a perfect site for their new hive on me, close to sweet buckwheat, just right in size. My brother ran away. I came home with 21 stings in my head. The room was twirling around, unfocused, barely visible through my swollen eyelids. When I fell asleep, I became a bee. There is a reason for it. 21 bees died to make me so.

curled in a flower
a bee dreams of honey —
sweetness at dusk

Dreaming Bees

What are the dreams of a bee, tucked away
in the safety of an orange blossom? The sweetness
of orange nectar soon to become golden honey?

Swimming in the ocean of sun-scented pollen?
Dancing in sunrays above orchards and meadows at sunset?

Earlier, I saw another bee asleep in my fragrant rose,
among rich magenta petals, wrapping her, like blankets,
in sweet dreams inside the Grande Dame of hybrid teas.

What are the dreams of this tranquil bee? Can we share them?
Can we, too, explore the vast, blooming fields of summer?
Pick nutrients off the stamens of peach flowers?

Soar, with translucent wings, high into the cupola
of pure sapphire, shimmering with air currents at noon,
darkening into indigo at dusk, speckled with starlight?

Oh, to be a bee! Peaceful, focused, fruitful, serene,
attentive—and resting within the abundant,
luxurious fragrance of star jasmine and roses—

Dreams of dreams—

A Pear in a Tree

By the sandy path
I climbed a pear tree
To watch the road
Melt into the horizon

I ate a golden pear
Juice stained my dress
My daydream of white
softness cut short
by the buzzing of wasps

They, too, longed for
The fruity sweetness
Of warm summer pears
They, too, dreamed
Of endless sunlight..

A Day Trip to Venice, California

The stunt kite traces the infinity sign
over and over above our heads in overcast sky
until it twirls into a spiral nose-dive and hits the sand
so hard it falls apart.

Again, it floats up — patiently, gently,
like wings of the dove, so steady high above us,
we fly up with our kite into the lucid, pearly milkiness
of clouds, shifting shapes on this strange afternoon.

A lone sailboat disappears into distance.
Pacific Ocean is cut in half by a sharply outlined pathway
of light leading towards the steely-white sun — so relentless
it pierces through the mist, carried onshore by winds.

We watch the stunt kite dance its dangerous dance.
Ominous cobalt waves turn into lead. Darkness falls

around us until we cannot see, only feel
the tug of outstretched lines that keep
the kite balanced in the air.

This is the trick of living well, this balance,
staying afloat on marine air currents
lifting us above — higher and higher
into pristine clarity — to postpone
the inevitable crash, avoid the death spiral
at all costs, any cost — live here and now
in the sweet by and by, on that beautiful shore,
singing the melodious songs
of the blessed —

Carving Sand

On the shore of the Pacific
a man carves out a sandcastle
with the straight, sharp edge of
a credit card. Crenellated ramparts,
tall arched gates, Gothic windows and
elaborate turrets — the castle comes into being
just for a moment — until the high tide washes it away
and the dream vanishes among the waves.

So do we — build our own sandcastles,
on credit, with cards we struggle to pay off
after darkness passes and the fog of despair
lifts up. Is it worth it? To keep the house for kids
and have no time to be there for them, with them?

Working, always working… Is it worth it?
To mortgage your whole future for a dream
of finding refuge in a rose garden, filled with
the sweetness of birdsong and orange blossoms?

Warm sunlight pours onto the beach,
outlines the carved contours of the sandcastle,
standing proudly alone, just for a moment,
for this moment, for us.

A Champagne Sunday

Moonlight. Sunlight.
Moonlight breeze. Upside down
half-moon in soft blue sky above us.

It is already four p.m., yet so bright on the
smooth, broad expanse of the beach in Oxnard –
white and sparkly as if the world were champagne.

We hold hands, jump in the waves,
of the Pacific – coming – coming – coming at us
with sprays of sea foam, saltiness of long-gone tears,
that will not return. I swear, they will not.

Each wave turns into a burst
of chilled, refreshing bubbly enveloping us
in sudden saltiness – stronger than the jolt of your sweat
dripping onto my lips last night, in our love's endless ocean.

The seawater shines with the translucent
aquamarine perfection of motion — motion — motion —

We float and twirl as effervescent bursts
of laughter flow smoothly, easily
off our lips, that know each other so well,
with the knowledge of years, ages even.

A full-hearted, full-throated laugh
of moonlight. Of sunlight. Of moonlight
breeze. Upside down half-moon
in soft blue sky above us.

Aquamarine

lucid
      lucent
            translucent
                   waves of the Pacific

 jade, turquoise, aqua

sea foam   in the air
      sea foam   on my skin

I dance on the currents
    floating with the relentless motion
   to the shore
         to the shore
                to the shore

sea foam
                        on my skin

          sea foam   in the air

Aphrodite comes up from the ocean

        carried on a dazzling shell by dolphins

                      the wisest of creatures

lucid
      lucent
            translucent

fizzy bubbles on my tongue —
       I swim in the champagne ocean
Salt of the Sol — sunshine of vitality
        I praise the elemental power of Water —
Air — Wind — Earth — Fire
        always Fire — *ogień*, Agni

eternal flames stir the waves

     into dancing

          to the shore
            to the shore

                  on and on

                          to the shore

                              to the shore

                                    to the shore

The Ocean of Jade

               spoke to me
                             yesterday

waves came to the shore
             to caress the sand
                      and paused in midair
                                    waiting for me to notice

        their smooth jewel surface
                their secret glow and the wisps
                       of white sea-foam twining through

             the air like lace on a collar
                      or an intricate shawl

            worn by an ancient
                        Lady Wisdom

the ocean of jade
            spoke to me —
                        look   and love
                                                look
            and   breathe
                                be   in awe

admire the infinity of magic
            jewels hidden and revealed
                        in one sweeping motion
                                    the same wave that came
to the shore
        to caress
                the sand
                        and paused
                                in mid-air
just for me

The 23rd of July

is the day of clearing karma
untying knots on the thread of fate,
breaking enchantments, reversing curses.

Look at the moon, blood-red and broken
above the hilltop, huge like ancient pain
passed on through generations.
It follows you, as you drive home
after resting in the silver mist of the ocean,
its waves — turquoise and jade — always
moving, yet always the same —

Look, the moon hides behind the black ridge
of despair, only a soft spot remains, shimmering
on alien indigo sky. The road turns, you fly along
80 miles per hour, singing a Chopin's Nocturne —
its lustrous cascade of notes split apart

by a sudden apparition — a majestic, white
platinum orb, suspended in darkness.

You remember that rust-red, once-in-the-lifetime
moon of prophecy, the fox moon that foretold
disaster as it led you back from Paso Robles, Solvang,
Santa Rosa, on the way into disillusionment and regret.
It was hard to understand. Harder to believe
in the existence of such twisted, demonic
selfishness masquerading as affection. Pitiful.

Yet the healing was real.
The lesson's learned.
The karma's cleared.
It is done.

The moon now floats high above the valley
in an eerie halo, distant and indifferent.
You've discovered the virtue of detachment.
You've seen how desires of the heart
led you astray. Your life — an illumination.

Like a moonbeam, glowing on cobalt waters
of the Pacific, your path ahead is straight — clear
— dazzling — brilliant —

A Starchild, born to shine, you are blessed
by the moon's radiance on this magical
summer evening of July 23rd. You are home.
The New Age has just begun.

Tatarak

A stand of water reeds, calamus, perfectly intact by the roadside.
How did it come here? *Tatarak* from a Polish lake grows at the edge
of dry, bronzed grass in California semi-desert. Green and healthy
It thrives in its new environment, like I should. I'm displaced, too.

Bathed in moonlight and flowing arpeggios of Chopin
Nocturnes, I speed along the freeway, escaping
from fiery flames and charred mountains
of human inferno. A survivor, I lived through
the entangled obstacles of fate, karma, disasters —
or rather, I should say , blessings — for they set me free,
unawares and confused, yet free.

Golden wings spread above my shoulder blades.
I soar into freedom, high above the ruined landscape
of my past, away from the fears of unknown future,
into the ever-widening gap of immeasurable present,
the eternity of NOW.

The growing, blooming, breathing is always NOW.
The plants so alive, spread out from their seeds.
Activated DNA creates patterns adjusted to
the persistent energy whorls, spirals.

How did the *tatarak* make it to California desert?
How and why did I? The twisted pathway of the past
does not matter. I'm blessed by light of the present.
Simply blessed.

Flying Kites

My kites respond faithfully to each tug of the string,
like pets on a leash. Sometimes, they wantonly resist
the pull, to crash-land on a brush-covered hillside.

The strange, geometric delta champion, with black-and-white
checkers on its chest, rainbow wings and tail, flaps its fins
as a flying fish that floats higher and higher, into the azure.

The swirling circle, a tribute to the ingenuity of unknown
engineers, is an air turbine, turning so fast that it seems ready
to power a lightbulb or open a portal to another universe.

The green baby dragon with red wingtips and streamers
capriciously turns here and there. Unstable, garishly hued,
it suddenly falls onto a thicket of dry chaparral bushes.

The golden macaw, enormous and silent, is so different
from its loud, obnoxious cousins. My parrot blissfully swings
from left to right, in an ethereal waltz of gold and red ribbons.

The laughing dolphin soars straight up — I look up to follow
the pathway of this magnificent guardian of the world,
crossing the ocean of air, so alive in the oxygen blue.

Flying kites is defying gravity. Flying kites is pure joy.
This is freedom itself, soaring towards the Sun,
circling around the Moon, tracing patterns among clouds.
My favorite is the simple diamond of colorful squares —
red, yellow, green, blue, violet — that shines in sunlight,
twirling on the end of its string, pointing the way home.

We used to make such diamonds of thin balsa wood
sticks and light parchment paper, our hands stained by glue.
The tail, a row of paper bowties on a string, undulated above
dark soil of potato fields, stretching to the horizon.

Flying kites is an apology for years lost to not being
little children that skip along the path, straight to heaven.
Flying kites is prayer, supplication, hymn of praise.

Flying kites is like love making to the air —
a dance of give and take — moving, shifting along
air currents that swirl above the hills at sunset.

It is like swimming in the air, below a violet butterfly
with wings outstretched on its ascent to the Sun, along
the pillar of light that connects the Earth and the Sky.

"Let me go!"
my kite tugs on the string —
we dream of freedom

Soap Bubbles

The sky is the color of soap bubbles
that Grandpa makes on the porch of old wooden house
in the village, the house with a peaked roof and three-panel
shutters on each window, closed only for winter storms
and departures, almost never —

The straws are tricky to make — of golden rye, cut between joints,
with the tip quartered and bent into a miniature cross of Malta.
We hold our straws gingerly, a solemn ritual of dipping them
in a dish of lukewarm water with a piece of brown soap,
then lifting the tips up and exhaling air slowly, carefully —
until the bubble, the soul of a plum or an apple,
detaches, becomes spherical, and floats away.

Iridescent, translucent, oscillating from pink, to blue, to gold,
to periwinkle, the sky at sunset is the color of soap bubbles.
I make a shiny sphere and watch its upward progress,
on a meandering path through warm summer sky, until
it bursts in a sudden gust of wind. The pang of disappointment
is real — it melts away only when another bubble is ready
to ascend on its random, weightless pathway. We count
them, one by one, keeping the score.

In times of trouble, make soap bubbles and watch them
float on air currents. Away. Into the unknown. The size
of a plum or an apple, iridescent, translucent, oscillating
from pink, to blue, to gold, to periwinkle. They float away,
specks of joy up in the sky — here just for a moment, until
they disappear in ever more distant, misty evening sky.

High Noon

All silent, we wait with bated breath
for the next word from the Great Sun —
a life changing utterance of grace and might

Everyone drinks in the brilliance
in this land of butterflies and birdsong, where
birds doze off, hidden among tree branches.
Radiant light caresses their backs.

We fall asleep drunk on luminosity and lightness.
Each one of us tightly wrapped in soft down
of cherubs, overshadowed by smooth angels wings.

It is so quiet now, at the high noon of summer.
Satiated, tranquil, serene — all dream in the arms
of sunlight. Their DNA codes are cleared and sorted.

Their cells fill with liquid light. There is no absence,
need, want, or sorrow. All is bliss — all peace —
all is perfect now — just now — right now.

Matka Boska Zielna

~ for Mother of God of the Herbs (August 15)

Look at the greening hill slopes charred by last year's wildfire—
that's magic. Look at the mountain sunflower that grew
at the edge of the asphalt on Oro Vista road, it already blooms
out of nowhere—that's magic, too. The postcard-size garden
by the old, wooden house, a shack, really—fills with flowers
every spring. Fruit appears on orange trees after bees collect pollen.

The scent of sweetness, the cheerful noise of bee wings—
is it not far more miraculous, a thousand, a million times
more delightful than the 100 floors of steel-metal-glass

of skyscrapers proudly pointing at the sky? Incomparable
with a patch of weeds, nature's miracles of renewal.

How proud we are of our empty metallic constructions
that will rust in the jungle, abandoned, like stone pyramids
of the Mayas, shrouded by vibrant green of leaves and
branches. Thousands of years of human fame obliterated
by the steady, living, fertile abundance, the overflowing
force of life, of matter, our Mother.

Roots, shoots, and tendrils spread out, germinate,
flow through the soil in search of water, nutrients,
life, more life, ever growing, ever richer, dancing,
singing the abundance of being — the song of creation
we are — we are — we are — we are all —
we are one — one — one —

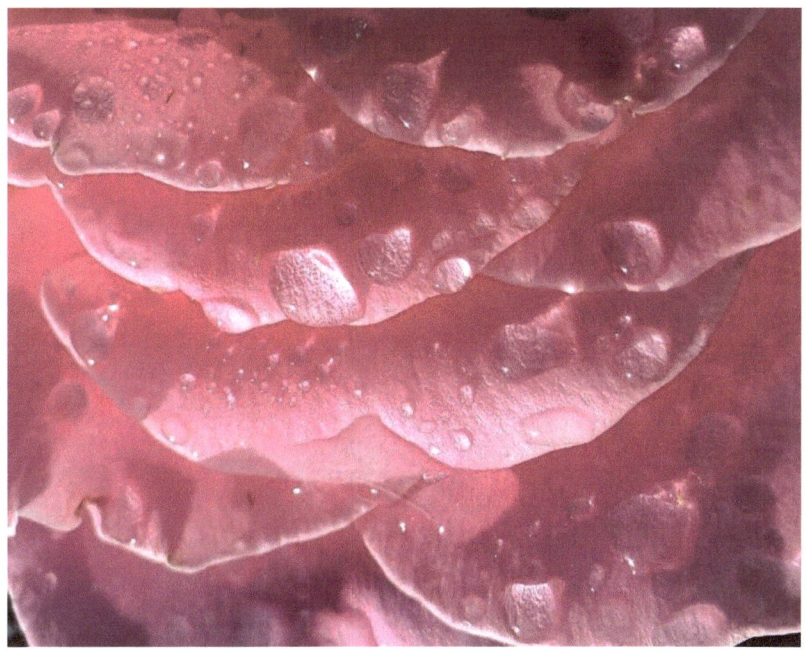

In Morning Light

We live on a planet where it rains diamonds —
hard rain, sparkling crystal droplets — in the clouds,
in the air, on the ground under our feet.
Here, the Valentine's Day falls on Ash Wednesday.
Red strawberries, wine-hot passion, and Ashes to ashes,
dust to dust — lessons of impermanence of the body,
constantly reconfigured in a vortex of quarks and atoms
until the pattern dissolves like snow at the end of winter.
Delicate snowdrops peek from under the melting cover
of phantasmagorical shapes and figures.

Here, the Annunciation Day of Mary's greatest joy
falls on Palm Sunday — from rainbow wings of Fra Angelico's
Gabriel bowing before the shy, blushing maiden in royal blue
we look ahead to the green of palm fronds lining the streets
of Jerusalem. We welcome the destiny of the King.
We see red blood on the stones of Golgotha,
the Place of the Skull. Not even this is real.
No wonder, then, that Easter, the greatest Mystery —
of Death into Life, Spirit over Matter, the Divine
in an emptied human shell — *Eli, Eli, Lema Sabachtani* —
Sanctus, Benedictus, Agnus Dei — it is done —
yes, that Easter — is on April's Fools Day this year.

We fool ourselves when we see death as enemy.
We spin our lives into thin filaments of a spider-web.
Illusion woven into illusion. Deception after deception.
They rise and fall with the rhythm of seductive charm.
The smiling demon is the most persistent. Incorrigible,
it pulls us down, down, down into the mud,
from whence we did not come. Nothingness
ties us up with bonds of non-being.

My revelation is this — we live on the planet
where it rains diamonds. We walk on untold treasures
that we do not notice — we forget and forget and forget
where we came from, where we are going.
 We spin our future out of spider silk and shadows.
Our lives fill with sand of dreams, changing
like shards of glass, broken bits of colored plastic
in a kaleidoscope — transfigured into the most
astounding waltz of the rosettes, reflected
in hexagonal mirrors of transcendence —

My revelation is this — we are the children
of sunlight — blessed by radiance — in love's
golden halos — we shine and blossom —
into a cosmic garden of stars — lilies — violets —

peonies — daffodils — and roses — always roses —
in this brilliant garden — on a diamond planet —
of what is — in the Heart of the Great, Great Silence —
— there's no here or there —
— there's no before or after —
— no inside or outside —
— — — All is Always Now — — —
— — — All is Always One — — —
— — — Where We Are — — —

NOTE: *with thanks to the Gospels, Giordano Bruno, St. Germain, and the strange calendar of holidays in 2018.*

BABIE LATO

On Thursday Afternoon

Your voice outside my window —
deep, calm flowing inexorably like a river
towards the future we will not know until
we look back and the past and say:
So that's what you meant. So, that's what it was.
Understanding the whole of the whole
that encircles us in a glowing sphere of
emotions — forgiveness, radiance, joy
of the fleeting moment, The present.

The golden line of a mockingbird song
weaves in and out of time — I follow
its ornamental thread into the present —
space opened up by gratitude
blossoming in a smile.

Sparrows in the birdbath, jet planes
in the sky, hummingbird's wings,
the dove's shadow passing over the lawn
and chimes playing endless variations
of the same melody over and over
until all time ends, and we are back
in that singularity beyond all spatiotemporal
emanations, back in One Love of One
Mind, One Will, One — Us.

Sapphire

My tiger orchid blooms again
for the third time already

It looks at me shyly
with topaz eyes

thinking, I'd remember
that night, that music
of togetherness —

*Expand, expand, forever
expand* — our hearts fill

with Cosmic Light of
a thousand Suns —

liquid and flowing
to heal and purify

We thank, we praise
the One Love

that blossoms
in emerald gardens

in sapphire flames
and bright tiger eyes

Amber

Red gold of falling leaves
and amber, liquid amber
engulf me with the intensity
of our love for all seasons —
Even the invisible California winter
without snow, with sunshine
and birdsong each morning — in time
for Darjeeling tea, Columbian coffee
and *naleśniki*, flat Polish pancakes
with a touch of maple syrup from Vermont.
The whole world celebrates with us
for we know the true meaning of attachment —
not the pink blush of infatuation —
not the wine-red rose of passion —
but this, only this — pure clarity
of azure skies — clear radiance of red gold
and amber — liquid amber

A Revelation After Il Paradiso

We live in the third sphere
of lovers, in the Earth's long shadow
Our love waxes and wanes
like the Moon, or Venus rising up
before dawn, the star of the morning
We oscillate from darkness to brilliance,
float from fear into sunlight
to rest on a golden afternoon
in the innocent warmth of affection
among newly planted roses
Imperial, Electric, Compassion
Double Delight and Simplicity roses

in our garden where we trim dried, twisted
branches of old oleanders to make room
for orange blossoms and more pomegranate
always more pomegranate
never enough pomegranate

Dark red translucent juice stains our fingers
Tart juice bursts with flavor
in our mouths, ready for kisses
always ready for more kisses
softest, childlike, strongest, tasting
like the wine we never tasted, the dream
we never even hoped to dream about
escaping the long shadow
of the Earth on a golden afternoon
lovers in the Garden of Love
afternoon in the Third Sphere of Venus
golden, golden, sparkling golden
afternoon from another planet

Up, Up, Up

With you, I'm a fairy-tale princess,
a Cinderella, perhaps, with her gold
spun-glass slipper on my nightstand
by the Polish Bible I use each day
to find out if I've been good.
I really do not know.

Sometimes, I'm a sleeping Beauty
with rosy cheeks, awakened
by the lightest touch of your lips.

Why are you my Prince Charming?
I really do not know. Why
did I have to cross the Great Plains
fly over oceans, wear out
three sets of iron boots, defeat
the Leviathan and the dark
Chameleon in my dreams?

Here I am—here we are
together. Step by step,
holding hands, we climb
the inaccessible heights of God's
white mountain, its snowy peaks
dazzling with the brilliance
of the sky—song—light—

From Yesterday's Dream

We are two foxes flying across the sky
with tails intertwined in gold and silver
of waning moon and pale sunlight.

We are two dolphins swirling, splashing through
the waves in aquamarine joy, seafoam — one more
one more again — let these waves never end —

until the salty sweat of the ocean carries us inland,
to the shore, we forgot exists, blessed beyond time.

We are the auspicious sign of double happiness —
two identical shapes outlined on scarlet silk satin.

We are two last pomegranates—red-ripe,
swaying in the breeze among golden leaves
that have started to fall. Winter's coming.

Brilliant, so full of promise, that tart sweetness
of nostalgia, dreams of unspoken loss—ready
to burst open, we wait for the destined hour
to turn into trees, to breathe in our carbon

to breathe out our *tlen*, to breathe in the sunglow,
to breathe out rays of subtle energy—permeating,
connecting us all in *miłość,* a vibrant cosmic lattice
that grows from the crystal seed of tomorrow.

NOTE *"Miłość" is love and "tlen" is oxygen in Polish.*

Sunfire Foxes

I come from a tribe of nine-tailed foxes
You are a gold fox with nine tails too

We splash in the pools of silver moonlight
We chase white stars through violet sky

We catch a ride on a sparkling comet
Nourished by nectar of honey dew

We leap through sunbursts, sunfire, sunrays
We rest in the golden glow of noon

Our wisdom grows in spirals, circles
Our joy is boundless, our love is true

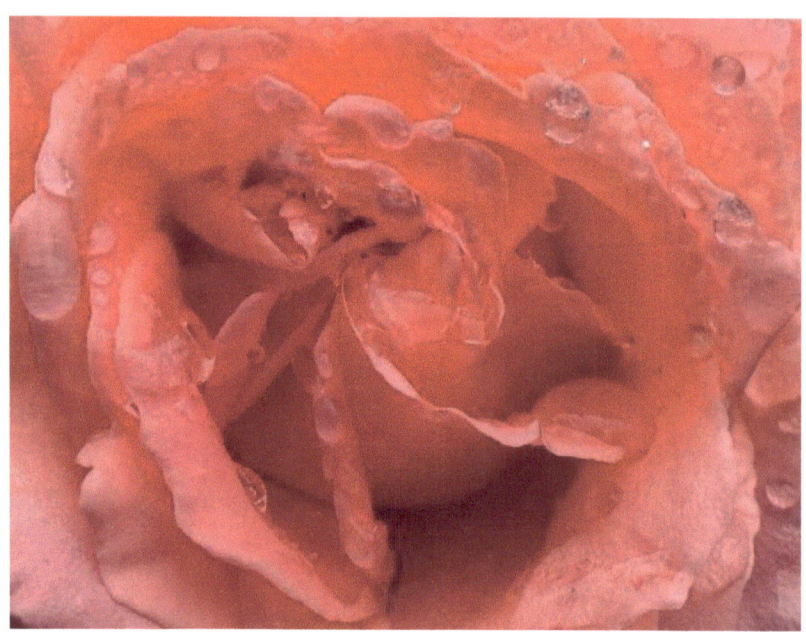

Sweet Nothings

We are the wings of a butterfly
Dancing in the vortex of time
Ascending to the heart of the galaxy
Flying higher and higher and higher

I love you. You love me.
I love you. You love me.
We are love, love, love, love
One love.

We are the wings of the butterfly
Twirling with a flutter in the breeze of time
Carried by currents beyond what's known
We swirl and rise up, together

I love you. You love me.
We are love.

What remains of the wings torn apart?
Is the pattern eternal? Does it stay
Once created and outlined in pure light,
embroidered on the fabric of reality
with a sparkling golden thread?

Yes, I love you. You love me.
I love you. You love me.
We are love, love, love, love
True love.

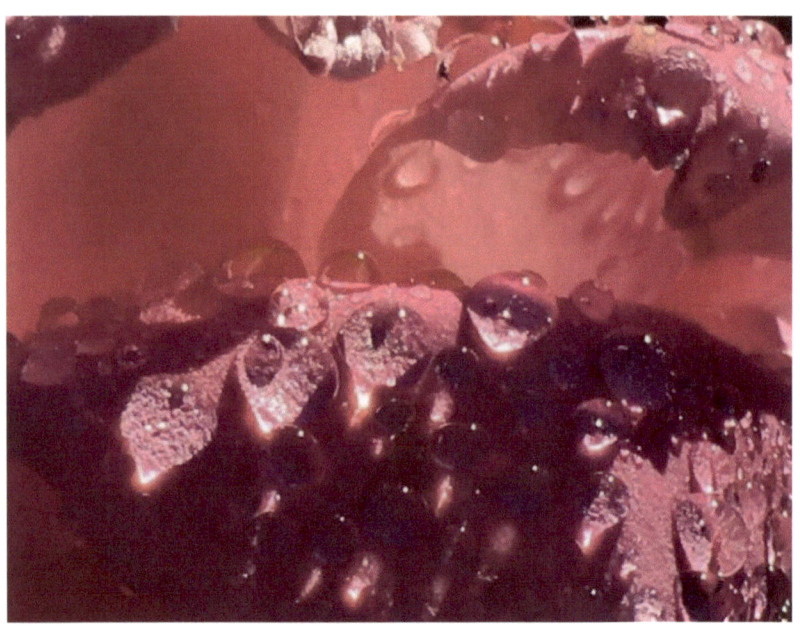

The Year of Crystal Fire

Soft patter of pink rose petals
falling onto the floor. The scent of French Perfume
in the air. The heartbeat stops. The world ceases its rotations.

I see the light in your eyes shining
through the slit in your motorcycle helmet,
as you pass me on the street. In a millisecond
of recognition you take me in — whole,
serene in turquoise and aqua — then, you look away
far into the past we shared so shamelessly,
beyond measure —
        the year of passion
        the year of dogs that brought us together
        the year of longing
        the year of dolphins dancing on salty waves
        the year of absence
        the year of waiting in darkness

    the year of tiger lilies
    the year of nine-tailed foxes—
        smooth with seduction and delight

Yes, I liked that year the most—
as we grew into our demonic, *daimonic* selves,
created new galaxies, parallel universes
out of our other-worldly love.

    Timelines shift.
    The cosmic windows
    keep opening and closing.
    Soft patter of pink rose petals
    on the flying carpet takes me into
        the year of passion
        the year of tiger lilies
        the year of diamond kites
        soaring above hilltops
        the year of stardust
        the year of crystal fire

Just to Make It Clear

Two falling stars in the day sky
~Hafiz

A woman is a sunburst shining in darkness.
A man is a sunray piercing the clouds.
The arrow flows straight into the heart of intention.
The wave envelops the world with pure Love.
Like a photon of Light—a particle, wave—
the two become One, the mystery Divine.
A woman, a man, two faces of brightness.
The radiance of starlight, so dazzling as One.
They blossom on petals of pure Divine Fire.
They float on unfolding wings of Divine Flame.
A woman, a man. Compassion and wisdom.
Light's pure revelation—a true cosmic gem

A Chromosome Ballad

The mothers of mothers of mothers
   plant seeds, care, and give birth.
     The fathers of fathers of fathers
        plant seeds, care, and protect.

     The mothers and fathers
       and sisters and brothers
          come here in organized waves.
          The mothers and fathers
        and sisters and brothers
          leave Earth after passing their tests.

When grandmas and grandpas have learned how to live,
   when moms, dads, aunts, uncles shared wisdom as if
     they each had a thousand-year-old treasure chest
     they could open with DNA keys at their best
        matched in pairs XX—XY, intertwined XX—XY
       strand after strand unwinding in pairs
    to give you your eyes of hazel or gray,
  your hair blond or brown, skin of varied hues,
your brilliance and talents, your gifts, and your moods.

     Remember the pathways
       they came on and left—
         the mothers and fathers
           of east and of west.

Twin Flame Promise

~to have, to hold, and to cherish
~ old English wedding vows

I take you to be my beloved
for today and tomorrow
for all days and nights
for a week and all weeks
for a month and all months
for a year and all years
for all eternity
wherever we are and will be
in rain and sunlight
in joy and happy togetherness
of our most holy marriage
our divine union
I promise you solemnly my love
faithfulness and honesty

and that I will not leave you until my death
I will be with you as long as I exist
I promise you the love of my heart
because you are my heart—
and the love of my body
because you are my body—
and the love of my eyes
because you are the light of my eyes—
and the love of my soul
because you are my soul mate
my being's other half
my fulfillment now and forever

In God, our Divine Source, Way, and Life
sharing our love for ever and ever

*And so let it grow and last and be
my promise for you and yours for me*

Diamonds

In a seashell there is an ocean
There is Universe within my heart
A myriad galaxies dance in my mind
I'm a microcosm of Divine design

In a seashell there is an ocean
In a dark coal mine white diamonds grow
In your eyes I find ageless wisdom
The One Love that sustains us all

In your guilt I see my darkness
In your beauty — radiance and light
In your voice — the calling, the calling

Mountain air on a spring morning
Sparkling diamonds, radiant and pure —
For all forevers you enfold me in Love

AUTUMN ~ JESIEŃ

On Cosmic Breath

Flowing, moving, liquid energy coalesces into
shapes, into lives, into beings of light, of earth
of solids and water. We are all One flowing, moving
liquid energy of ether, spirit, light; spilling over
limits, borders, obstacles, dark walls of separation.

Spilling into connection, convergence, unity.
Cosmos breathes in waves of energy — endless, insistent,
relentless, they inexorably swell and recede over aeons of time,
always moving, always here — flourishing, moving, liquid
energy of the Source — Light — Love — Life.

On Landscapes: A Guidebook

First you cross the Salt Plains of Rejection
into the Desert of Abandonment.
Mount Disappointment lies just beyond
The Valley of Regret. This is a huge country.
You lived there for decades. You explored
every nook and cranny; path, boulder, crevice.

Ever since your mother disappeared
for five months and a year. Ever since
you learned to write at six to send her
your desperate pleas: "Mommy, come back.
Mommy, I love you. Mommy, why don't you
love me, anymore?" You re-lived this story
time and time again. In every marriage, romance.

Now you know too well how it feels.
Now you can open the enchanted book
and say the words of magic.

You pour out a River of Molten Light—
dazzling, white hot, yet cool to touch—
over the chaff of broken feelings, the dust
of memories you wish were not yours
to keep and gather for the Ancient One.

The chaff burns.
The shadows flee.
You find a grain of gold
Under your feet.
Smooth, shiny, polished,
It is yours to keep.

Is it a grain? Look closer, a golden acorn
rests in the palm of your hand. Plant it
in Guilt Valleys. Plant it in the Deserts
of Despair. plant on Fear Mountain slopes.
Plant on wind-swept Plains of Sorrow.
It sprouts so fast. Soon, a magnificent oak tree
spreads out its gold leaves and boughs.
New life in your Landscape of Desolation.

Look through its branches. Be mindful,
attentive. What do you see?

Here — the Fertile Fields of Bonding. There —
the Rainbow Meadows of Connection.
Look carefully now. See the Pristine Peaks
of Fulfillment, the Sun Garden of Gratitude?
Filled with every kind of fragrant blossoms,
the heady perfume of rose and jasmine,
the delicate scent of lavender and forget-me-nots.
Liquid melodies of birdsong in the air.
This is not a mirage. This is your world
to conjure up, and delight in.
Here. This gold grain is for you.
Will it become an acorn or
a pinecone in your hand?

Come, let's plant it.
Watch it grow.

A Cosmic Rainbow

Blue—cornflower, azure, sapphire, indigo
sky, sky, sky, sky of Divine Mind. Sky.
Infinite expanse, clear and translucent sky
calls to us, waits for us to plunge into
its hidden depths, to awaken.

Green— jade, moss, forest, emerald, fronds,
grass, leaves, stems, fruit of the Divine Heart

of the Earth—fertile, abundant, teeming
with life Earth surrounding us with blessings.
Earth calls to us, waits for us to taste
its heavenly nourishment, to care for
the perennial growth , to awaken.

Gold—yellow, daisy, aster, finch, sand,
sunlight of time, transition, energy flowing
from shape to shape, life to life, forming, dissolving
building up, falling down—an eternal flow of energy
power, life—calls to us, waits for us to be,
to become, to expand, to awaken.

Red—ruby, garnet, rose-petal, wine, blood,
my blood, your blood flowing through the veins
of Divine Body, carrying oxygen and food
into all the cells, all the microscopic beings
that come together, to be me, to be mine,
to serve the Gold, Green, Blue and Violet.

Violet—royal purple, amaranth, amethyst,
iris, rainbow, flame—dancing, twirling in spirals,
flying upward, connecting, linking all into
a cosmic lattice of timeless presence—calls to us,
waits for us, to weave its liquid strands,
to pleat its living braids, to ascend into being,
into the white, awakened.

White—camellia, lily, daisy, snow, quartz, diamond,
the spark of light broken off the infinite pyramid
of Divine Will, sent out into the Red, Gold, Green
Blue and Violet—to explore, to experience,
to live, to breathe, to cry, to laugh, to gather
the fruit and bring them back—untouched
and uncensored, fruit of life, my life in white.

Today – For Us

We are a miracle of life

We do what we want
We want what we do

We are perfect

We are cosmic trees
We grow by the calm lake of light

Its smooth opal surface
Reflects the sun's smiling face

Our roots drink liquid light
Our crown sparkles with stars
Our leaves are green with peace

Our flowers are gold with joy
Our fruit is ripe with wisdom

We are a living miracle
We are perfect

From noon to midnight
From midnight to noon

We love what we do
We do what we love

We are — we shine —
We are one with the One

We are perfect

I Give You the World

> *~ for the birth of my first grandson, Adam, September 2016*

I saw you
with eyes closed, smiling
among waves, shadows
changing direction—
where are you?

Adam, the first man,
I give you the whole Earth
to name.

I give you my world with veins of gold
slicing through the drab clay of hours,
drops of amber hidden in sand,
turquoise among slabs of granite,
and pure diamonds in charcoal.
I give you rocks in the riverbed,
white, grey, and veined with pink—

so you step on the solid foundation
and grow up with both feet on the ground
strong and stronger each day.
I give you water laughing in the stream,
so your laughter spills over
the waves of air, lightly, in silvery droplets.

I give you the hummingbird's feathers ruby-
red and emerald green—
their feisty owner suspended in mid-air
on invisible wings, drinking nectar
from birds of paradise and a butterfly-shaped
bougainvillea in the intense shade of magenta.

I give you the patience of a lizard, sunning itself
on my pathway, and catching flies—
no, I do not give you the gift of catching flies,
or maybe… it could be useful!
Well, let's stay with the virtue of patience
of waiting for the right moment—do everything
at the right time—do everything right.

You may like the intense hue of the California poppy
a wildflower of the hills. As orange as laughter,
with delicate green leaves of the spring, it comes back
year after year, without rain, soon after fires.
Like this poppy, please, never give up!

I give you the riches of the clear, crisp air
in the fall, when gingko, maple, and poplar
leaves turn yellow and crunchy under your feet,
when last peaches get wrinkly and too sweet
on half-empty branches in the orchard.

I give you the heady scent of needles
on Christmas tree, a Douglas fir covered
in handmade ornaments, hidden behind
a mountain of gifts in crinkly wrapping paper,
green, red, gold, and navy — next to a row
of stockings waiting for chocolate on the mantel.

I give you the chirping of the cricket
behind my chimney — their summer song,
the kind my Grandma heard in the freezing,
snowy winter in Trzebieszów. I wish you
always have a cricket behind your chimney.

Let it sing, if it wants to sing!

I give you the majesty of sequoias, tall and ancient
with heads in the sky, roots stretching down,
inter-connected. Solid, immobile, above and beyond
it all. Theirs is the gift of nobility, strength and resilience.
They do not die in forest fires—just get singed and grow
new branches—that's what I give you today.

When you grow taller, I'll give you wings
to fly in planes, across oceans to distant cities—
London, Paris, Rome, the City of Angels,
to the white coral sand under coconut palms
on Pacific islands, and to the waterfalls
and volcanoes of Hawaii. Come on! Grow up! Let's go!

We'll enter magnificent cathedrals
and listen to angelic voices and heavenly
sawing machines of Johann Sebastian Bach.
We'll climb the world's most famous tower
to look down at the rooftops and streets,
Eating ice-cream, and almonds, and *crêpes*.

I give you the rush of understanding,
the "aha" moment when you get it
and things fall into place where they
should have been from the start.
Stuffed into this junk heap of ideas
is a gift of making cosmos from chaos
in the pristine, strong light of your mind.

And don't forget the white kernel
of fresh walnut after you peel off its yellow
wrinkly skin. All the bitter flavor is gone,
only sweetness remains—just like in life,
when lived right. So, yes, I give you the true gift
of living right, capturing each moment
and dissecting it into what to keep
and what to discard.

My gift is unique and hidden.
You'll find it inside you, when your bare feet
touch the new grass and your eyes follow
shifting clouds in the blue-grey Polish sky.
This is the gift of knowing what is true,

how grass grows, how clouds become scarves for
hilltops. How to be present to changing sunlight
on the mountain slopes with patches
of shadow moving through distant canyons
and meadows. This is my gift.

So, my dear first-born grandson, son of
my first-born son, I give you the colors,
scents, and flavors of fall, winter, spring
and summer. Know that what becomes old
dies out, letting new flowers blossom into
the delicious fruit of experience and memory.

I never thought of memory as a jar of pickled pears
with cinnamon sticks and cloves, ready for
a winter feast. Apparently, that's what it is.
Thus, I give you some pickled pears of your
Grandma, great-Grandma, and greater great-
Grandmas, with family recipes and stories to keep.

I give you the bells of sailboat tack, ringing

against the mast on your boat in the harbor,
waiting for another adventure on undulating
grey waves of a lake. That's for a summer day.
For winter nights, I give you ten billion suns
in each of ten billion galaxies as your playground.
You will find your way from sun to sun.

I give you hand-written letters, spirals
of sunflower seeds, a snail shell, and
the cycle of seasons, living breath of our planet.
Please accept mysterious ancient maps, fractal veins
on a rose petal and on tributaries to rivers
you will see from the orbit through electronic
machine eyes. I give you the multitude of seeds
in a pomegranate, each seated in its own
ruby-red pod, squished into the tightest space.

This is how tightly knowledge will be packed
into the neurons and cells of your brain,
so, you can squeeze its sweetness into words
of supreme wisdom.

I give you the gift of my language, many languages,
really—two for certain, maybe three, four, five, or six
I could have spoken if I tried harder, made more time.

So now you can do it—learn more skills, get more
knowledge, expertise. Let's not forget beauty, the true
meaning of life—see the snowflake star crystals
melting on your glove? That's being like the lilies
of the field clothed in glory, lilies that stretch their heads
to the sun, breathing in, absorbing the golden essence
of life with each leaf, root, and petal. So, there.

I wish for you the murmur of waterfalls
and the silver resonance of Tibetan chimes,
slowly swirling through the evening air
with the smoke of frankincense or sweetness of jasmine.
I wish you to be wrapped in a halo of light-filled
silence and surrounded by the sparkling notes of music
that'll keep you shielded in a gold armor against the dark.
I wish, I wish, I wish for you the most precious gift
of loving-kindness, a grand river of luminescent calm
flowing through every hour of your peaceful life.

I give you all the beautiful and good things I find.
What you do with my gifts is yours only —
store them in the treasure chest of allotted time
to do this and that, or this much, or just enough.
May every step lead you to higher awareness,
compassion for all living beings, greater wisdom,
and more intense connection with all others —
plants, animals, people. May your song echo widely
across Cosmos. May you learn to sail, swim, climb
mountains, build, paint, or plant — as you wish.
May each day be full of hours shining like
peacock's feathers, in an open fan of delight.

I give you the invisible secret — cords of light tying
all beings together — plants, stars, oceans, tree roots
and clouds. Warm softness of the nose of a puppy
or a baby kitten — would you like dogs or cats?
And a myriad of happy eyes, looking at you
with the warmth of affection — like mine.

Don't forget where you came from
and why — to link, connect, span the globe

and shine, yes, shine. May the beautiful luster
of your un-excelled essence, be known among
millions of suns, in dazzling star crowns—
like Buddha's supreme joy, and the lotus
of wisdom, dissolving into clear light.

If you are an artist, make a living,
be grateful for your gifts, and give back
in kind. If an engineer, invent things
to help people, or animals, or plants.
If a healer, may you heal people, soil, water,
and air. Make them happy, hear their song—
that's what we want most of all. To be
heard, to be cherished, to be loved.

When you choose, choose wisely
and follow your heart,
always follow your heart.

A Golden Poem for the Girl of Gold

~ for my granddaughter, Aurelia, in September 2021

I gave Adam, your brother, the whole world,
when he was born in Poland. What is left for you?

When you grow up, will your hair shine
soft and gold, cascading in waves over your
suntanned shoulders — Rapunzel style?
Will your smile have an effervescence
of angel wings from Fra Angelico's frescoes —
a touch of otherworldly joy?

Will you like as much as I do the turquoise
and gold flower ring my dad found for me
In Mosul, Iraq? Or the Russian sapphire
engagement ring of my Mom, your great Grandma?
The precious stone all scratched up in a lifetime

of love's labor — the ring never taken off
while sewing, cooking , washing dishes?
The precious ring of married love.

Will you cherish the gold filigree butterfly
pendant from Grandma Henia, my gift
for your Mom, an heirloom for you —
as much as I admire the real butterfly
hovering to drink nectar from hibiscus
and rose blossoms? Its golden wings
fluttering in the stillness of high noon?

You are so small now. You do not know yet.
I do not know either. You will choose
what you love. It is all gold anyway,
if you look through golden glasses
and awaken the magic world
within your own heart of gold.

Gold Wishes

~ for the birth of my first granddaughter

Aurelia, the golden name glowing like an aureole
of saints and Madonnas on ancient altars,
intricately patterned to bedazzle the eyes
of believers, unlock their hearts.

Gold does not tarnish, rust or fade — timelessly
shining in the crowns of Egypt, India, Sarmatia.
Gold wedding rings on your parents' fingers
do not fade either, as they tie them together
for a lifetime of love, shared in kind.

Baroque gold frames around paintings we treasure
reflect light and make the images within
even more startling — like Van Gogh's harvesters
resting in golden fields of Provence at noon
while grayness spreads out in the rainy Paris.

You look at yourself in a gold-framed mirror.
What do you see? The pure gold of innocent laughter?
The gold of serene silence that shimmers
just for you? Look deeper, find the golden soul
within the soft light — the perfect, lovely YOU
of brilliant effervescence, incandescent charm.

Listen to the golden notes of birdsong
falling from the sky onto the gold carpet
of gingko leaves surrounding the ancient tree,
a symbol of long and healthy life, that I wish for you,
a shower of blessings under your feet.

Close your eyes. Smell the delicate fragrance
of Oregold rose, sparkling morning dew,
droplets scattered like diamonds
on yellow petals.

Taste the gold of honey, each teaspoon
a lifework of a single bee, that flew 30,000 miles
gathering pollen to nourish and heal.

Relish the sweetness of small golden grapes
you pick off a trellis in Grandma's garden—
ripened with elements from earth, water, air, fire
they fill you with contentment and grace.

Let gold afternoon sunrays dance and split
into rainbows under your eyelids. Breathe in
the gold of sunlight. Breathe out the gold of love.
I am sending you the abundance of blessings.
Remember, for your whole life, be a true child of gold.

Juniper

~ for the birth of my second granddaughter, September 2021

J

Jun

Juni

Juniper

is the name of surprise

a mysterious guest that comes

to shine with joy and explore delights

of knowing, hearing, seeing, touching, tasting

gifts, flavors, sounds, sights, scents, sensations

unseen, unheard of, unlikely — discovered in

four wild deserts and eight distant seas,

blessed with the wondrous presence

in the here and now

Juniper

Juni

Jun

J

The Fierce Explorer

~ For my granddaughter, Juniper, in April 2022

Look into hazel eyes of this intrepid explorer
venturing into the world with curiosity and courage.
Exploring plants, toys with hands and tongue.
Climbing over the obstacle course of pillows
into a laundry basket or a flower bed.
Dipping toes in the cold waves of the Pacific.
Tasting sweet, sour, salty, and spicy flavors of life.

The eyes are the mirror of the soul, they say.
You were so tired after the ordeal of your passage
into this life, so exhausted. Now, sparkling, wide open,
your eyes are filled with ever-growing joy.

Nurtured by patient affection of your parents,
you are sustained by the blue-green energy arc of love,

guiding you to explore all the good things in life.

Your name, Juniper, takes you into the wild,
wild forests of America, ancestral Canada, and Poland.
A landscape adorned with green flames of graceful
bushes bearing blue berries, a favorite savory spice
of your great Grandma Henia and Grandpa Alek.

Picked in the forest in Bielewicze, kept in a jar
on a Warsaw kitchen shelf, on the tenth floor of
a gray apartment block, so far from forests, so close
to blue skies. Juniper berries are the key spice for *bigos*,
a recipe for hunter's stew passed on through generations.

The dark-green needles, the hue of chlorophyl,
the color of plant love for us, fill the air with oxygen
for our lungs. Breathe deeply, my dear, go on, explore,
with every breath, every taste, every song.

The Aril

"Aril" is the word for me.
Not "arid"—as in the desert of wasted years, hours.
Not "arduous"—as in working so hard every day
to make ends meet. These ends, they never meet, anyway.

Just aril. As in my garden at noon. As in ruby-bright
pomegranate shining in full sunlight. A jewel bowl
of arils I pick from exploded fruit to freeze for winter.
A handful of overripe arils that taste rejuvenating,
like fine wine. Tartly sweet juice stains my fingers
burgundy-red—or should I say, aril-red?

Oh, the delight of untold riches!

You watch me blissfully chew the seeds
and say in disbelief: "You eat them whole? Really?
When I was a boy, my brother told me that
trees would grow out of my ears if I swallowed

pomegranate seed — huge trees would grow
and grow and grow and grow…"

We laugh at the vision of these arid, forgotten years.
It was an arduous journey that took us through
the wilderness to this vivid moment of sharing
this magic, life-giving nectar of arils,
ruby-red arils.

Fall Yucca

Golden stems shine like beams of sunset
piercing the purple valley that sinks
into darkness under a soap-bubble sky.

The stems lean sideways, imperceptibly falling
these are our leaning towers of Yucca in the desert
valley that I make my home. I breathe deeply, delighted

by the omnipresent sheen and sparkle of sonorous
cicadas that rush to surround me with their scintillating
songs of summer, before rains silence them into sleep.

Long, narrow yucca leaves gather at the stems
like supersonic star-beams meeting at one point
on the horizon, blurred by velocity of a Star Wars flight.

They burst out at dusk with a silvery glow
of moonlight — then detach from their drying stems
to crumble into the thick charcoal of the earth.

The yucca's white lily flowers have long turned into
bunches of seed-pods — waiting to fall and germinate
into spikes of sharp leaves that poke from the rocky soil

with a promise and a certainty of survival —
the next year's yucca. Shadows reveal sparks
of icy stars above me — I walk home, content.

This Evening

It will be that way but for a moment—the light is dying
now as sunset dissolves into nightfall. The sky is the hue
of soap bubbles—orange to pink to celadon and pearl
gray, with cloud stripes, below an expanse of periwinkle,
a cupola ready to burst open.

The hues are more seductive, for there is smoke in the air,
the scent of dying trees, grass, bushes perishing in flames
somewhere to bring us their last offering. We watch
the sky glowing like soap bubbles—vivid, shifting, lucent.

Are we the most alive at the edge of dying? The most
attuned to living after we are told we have a year,
or maybe a month to put things in order? We admire
the maples and ginkgo trees covered in splendor
of scarlet and gold just before leaves fall. This is the sign
of passing, a farewell to their happy life.

Aren't the iridescent hues of the sky telling us
that we still have time, so little time, yet time enough
to fully immerse ourselves in this moment, to reach
the zero point of here and now and be aware of its beauty?

We are content under the translucent sky of orange, gold,
silver and periwinkle, half-way between blue and violet,
just as we are half-way between life and death,
body and soul, heart and mind—suspended on an invisible
silver thread from the galaxy's web. One neuron
in the enormous mind of all stars, all beings, all trees,
all molecules of air and light. So much light!!!

Diamond Rain

We live on a planet
where it rains diamonds
on red-gold leaves of myrtle tree
under the azure sky so alive that it breathes
and vibrates in the distance.

Look up! See the cosmic sigh?

We live on a planet
where it rains diamonds.
Water droplets shine in sunlight
scattered on pine needles and broad leaves
of the bird of paradise, stretching, stretching,
growing until orange blossoms alight amidst the foliage
like a flock of birds, copper flames in jade.

On my planet, western bluebirds,
finches, and doves drink from the fountain.
They fly away when the scrub jay comes to take a bath,
dip his head into the water and shake diamond droplets
down his back.

On my planet, hummingbirds hum
suspended in the air by red hibiscus flowers.
Mockingbirds mock the tune of my alarm clock
at four a.m. and sing the songs of redwing blackbirds
that pass through on the way to Mexico or Canada
resting in the garden, then moving on.

My planet, where it rains diamonds,
breathes and vibrates with wave after wave
of energy that spins into life forms, growing, decaying, returning—
the endless ocean of live diamonds
that multiply and sparkle in the sun.

WINTER ~ ZIMA

California Winter

White snow powders the distant mountain tops
sparkling in morning sun like icing on Gaia's cake.
I drive and drive seeking the purity of cold water.
My mountains, worn down to hills, closer, are golden brown,
with their contours sculpted by shadows on rims and gullies,
decorated with olive-grey sage and bronze-green manzanita.

It is not easy to find solace in these hills, not even
when the sky, free of chemtrails, is clear sapphire
infinity, shimmering with the endless joy of sunlight.
Not when I, looking up at the snowy beauties high above,
Step on slippery wet soil and mud encases the soles of my boots.
I shiver, chilled by a sudden gust of winter breeze.

On my quest for clarity, I drive through rocky canyons,
raining boulders onto the road, my destination further
and further away. Yes, the air is clearer here, silence rings.
The unknown mountain bird calls me to go on and on,
to find the treasure that glows all around me—alive,
so alive, with the mud and manzanita, sage, and snow.

I arrive at the Big Tujunga Dam Overlook. Finally,
the majestic peaks appear before me. I find a dime
on the ground. Rocks, the hues of cyan, rust and bone
disintegrate into pebbles, grains of sand scattered
beneath my feet. One day, I will become a jewel,
while my body turns into sand under calm water.

Standing In a Pool of Silver

In an ocean of bronze at sunset,
I'm waiting for the tide to turn,
for the moon to show us
its dark side.

I know this light is mine—
silver, sparkling, platinum,
it surrounds and protects me
against an onset of metallic bronze.

The ripples of the surface
change quickly,
bronze melts into the dark.

I'm standing in a pool of silver.
It shines, it sparkles, it glows.

The Antidote

Chaos breaks out in our cities full of noise,
toxins, radiation. I withdraw into my garden,
compress the sphere of attention,
intensifying the focus on minute details.

The liquid patterns of finches' song, repeated
like a broken record. The sediment lines
on the layered rock from Big Tujunga Wash.
The translucent opal of a quartz stone,
smoothed by the Pacific on Oxnard Beach.

The imperceptible motion of leaves
expanding skywards, while their roots
stretch down invisibly, moist with dew.

Is it not enough to taste a pomegranate,
really taste each tart aril, bursting in your mouth?
Is it not enough to turn your face up,
to be kissed by noon sunlight?

"No fear, no hate, not even a slight dislike"
says St. Germain. I clear the rubble
of memories of past pain, stronger,
more clingy than the pain itself.

The mind is full of useless knowledge.
The body remembers on its own.
Pitiful. The heart locks itself
in a hard shell of protectiveness.

I have to conquer this chaos within,
polish lamps, wash the windows
into sparkling translucence, letting
the light in—the antidote to chaos.

A Music Box Christmas

      I wind the spring on the music box.
      Silvery specks swirl in the snow globe.

The twinkling of "We wish you a Merry Christmas"
fills the air. Santa on the rooftop falls into the chimney.
Are you ready for the holidays? With Scottish whisky cake,
Polish *makowiec*, American apple pie? Will you cook
Tamales on Christmas Eve, your family gathered
Around steaming pots, laughter mixed with hearty flavors?
Will you roast turkey with fixings on Christmas Day?
Will you nibble slices of chocolate oranges, unwrap gifts?
Will you taste walnuts and sesame snaps from your stockings?

      I wind the spring on the music box.
      Silvery specks swirl in the snow globe.
      Memories of home swirl before me.

I make cranberry sauce with pears and apples
the way my Mom taught me. Do I still know
how to chop figs and dates into finely ground
poppy seeds boiled in milk, re-fried with honey?

Family recipe for *kutia*. The favorite flavors
of childhood, float away with Ogiński's polonaise,
Farewell to the Homeland. Under blazing California sun
I still taste the exotic desserts of Poland's eastern lands,
where cultures mixed and worlds mingled — Poles,
Lithuanians, Tartars, Jews. Cornflower blue skies,
shimmering gold of rye fields.

>   I wind the spring on the music box.
>   Silvery specks swirl in the snow globe.
>   I make a promise to myself I will not break.

This Christmas, I'll read a novel, wrapped in
a plush red blanket and a Santa hat. I will walk alone
in the park, come back to the empty house and watch
The Lord of the Rings, the epic battles of the elements,
good versus evil, good versus evil, forever.
The silvery specks dance in the snow globe.
I sing along "We wish you a Merry Christmas"
and I think of a Christmas play in Canada with
my four-year-old Angel Ania waving a pine bough,
singing with a chorus of children's voices,
"We swish you a Merry Christmas
and a Happy New Year!" Let them swish…

Rules for Happy Holy Days

Don't play Christmas carols
at the airport. Amidst the roar
of jet engines, they will spread
a blanket of loneliness over the weary,
huddled masses, trying not to cry for home.

Don't put Christmas light on a poplar.
With branches swathed in white galaxies,
under yellow leaves, the tree will become
foreign, like the skeleton of an electric fish,
deep in the ocean.

Clean the windows from the ashes
of last year's fires. Glue the wings
of a torn paper angel. Brighten
your home with the fresh scent
of pine needles and rosemary.

Take a break from chopping almonds
to brush the cheek of your beloved
with the back of your hand,
just once, gently. Smile and say:
"You look so nice, dear, you look so nice."

A Ballad from the Field of Glory

Last night I was mobbed by monsters,
Surrounded from all sides in the dark.
Crowds seethed to the distant horizon—
Steel fangs, claws, charcoal eyes.

I said:
"Be patient.
Please, wait in line.
I'll get to you, I promise."
And so, it began.

I laid my hands on their foreheads.
I laid my hands on their hearts.
I breathed light into their nostrils.
I kissed their opaque third eyes.

One by one, they began dancing.
One by one, they started to laugh.
"We were curious," they said, "you're fearless,
We came to see what it was about."

I smiled at my new disciples —
Tall lizards, crocodiles, baboons,
A pack of sharp-toothed midnight foxes
And a horde of dark, shaggy wolves.

Men with strange, dark wooden faces,
Empty eyes of pure absence, so vile,
A vulture with a bald neck, and two sharks —
I worked on them ceaselessly all night.

I called my companions to help me,
To share their true breath of life.
First, Spinek, spider-crab of clear diamond,
Once curled at the root of my spine.

He makes cartwheels of joy, high above me,
With Naguska, gold snake, jewel eyes.
Sent to hurt me, fill me with poison,
She now uses her fangs to inject light.

Misiek, my honey bear is close by.
Milky Koala holds onto his back.

They stretch, shake off sleep from their fur coats.
Go to work, breathing, sharing the light.

Nine-tailed Foksik comes late, as always.
Smooth platinum fur sparkles with stars.
Free to do as she pleases, she binds them
Firmly, to Divine Love, Divine Light.

Now, I stand in the midst of my army.
Waves of laughter pass through the ranks.
Their happiness flows to the horizon.
The aura of joy fills the night.

I'm the Queen of Angels, of Cherubs.
I'm Sovereign, above Host of Hosts.
We are gentle, loving. In kindness,
Living water springs from all hearts.

Invincible, we shine with pure glory.
United, we waltz, and we dance.
"What of monsters?" You ask. Let me tell you,
"Angelic, we are all born of Light."

A Jewel Box Sunrise

Silver cirrus clouds float west
like shoals of fish in an amethyst sky.
Sun rises over a wintry orchard.
The smooth Zeppelin of poetry
carries me above the tangle of dreams.
I rest, bruised after stumbling
through twisted roots, broken tree limbs.
Frost grows flowers on windowpanes.
See how they dance? You nod
over your morning tea. "You are welcome,"
I smile at your questioning gaze.
My Grandma's gold-rimmed *filiżanka*
warms your hands. Steam rises
from the bright topaz liquid.
"Tea flows in your veins, sweets,"

you say, laughing. The helium of words
fills the skin of the moment.
"Come here," you say, wrapping
your arms around my waist.
A kiss of herbal fragrance.
Dawn blossoms into lucid light.
We go outside, stand under
Snow-covered cherry trees.
They sigh and crackle. Their sap
rises deep beneath the bark.
The white balloons of our breath
dissipate through cold air crystals.
Having waited so long, I'm glad
for my jewel box sunrise.

NOTE: "filiżanka" means porcelain teacup in Polish.

Winter Solstice

Remember, I'm not your
girlfriend — I am your interstellar
wife — you, my interstellar husband

We meet in clouds above
clouds, beyond violet sunrise
Hand in hand, we float into infinity

We hold paired spheres of brightly
polished copper and glowing amber
smooth as honey — for harmony
and balance of body and soul

We become stronger
more aware each day

Affection explodes into twin flames
dancing through galaxies, tightly
intertwined — round and round, again —

Ascending into crystalline whiteness
above star orchards, we pass through
fragrant blizzards of swirling dogwood
petals and cherry blossoms

Crowned with timeless jewels,
we are the most serene prince
and princess of interstellar flight

The Star of Christmas, the Way of Light

Jupiter and Saturn became one. Distant
orange gold merged with deep blue purple
into a diamond white Bethlehem star.
A solstice miracle.

    We saw it through the telescope
    in the neighbors' driveway.

The cross on the hilltop is flooded with light.
A Christian beacon, a sea lantern on the shores
of receding darkness. The end of Kali Yuga,
the twisted age of destruction and chaos.

    We look at it from the safety of our bed—
    limbs intertwined, after interstellar flights
    through galaxies of affection.

The portal opens. The way back
irrevocably closes. From the Zero Point
of no return, we step into the Age of Aquarius.
my Winter Solstice poem comes to life.

   Togetherness, acceptance carry us
   on ultraviolet waves into
   the ultramarine infinity
   of one true love.

Our ascent is punctuated by sudden
bursts of laughter, flavored
with the sweetness of winter tangerines,
dissolving into the pure intensity
of childlike joy — rediscovered
at the threshold of the Golden Age,
embroidered on the fabric
of the Thousand Years of Peace.

Gifts

> *...the necklace of songs, that you take as a gift*
> *~ Rabindranath Tagore*

I gather sunlight
in my palms
to save for later
when it's dark outside
and hope seems lost.

My hands are full
of brightness.
I gingerly carry
the tangle of sunrays
in a procession of gifts,
down the aisle.

I gather sunlight
to keep close
to my heart,
and warm us
through cold
winter nights
with a rich glow
of sunfire.

New Year's Day in the Wash

Dry riverbed, waiting for rain,
glows with yellow leaves — ash, cottonwood,
and poplar — sparkle in afternoon sunlight.

A stream of gold flows along steep hillslopes
of charcoal rocks and sparse, russet bushes.
Is it still chapparal if it grows on the incline?

Would I use acid, chrome, or imperial yellow, or perhaps
minium from medieval manuscripts, if I were a painter,
able to capture this splendor on my canvas?

The golden river of autumn leaves illuminates
the canyon. After twenty-five years in California,
I'm surprised by this opulence of sudden riches.

Like a three-month-old baby I look at the world
with round, open eyes — *What is it?* and
What is that? and *What is this?*

Clouds, trees, people — what are these shapes,
sounds, sensations? The mystery of seeing
that matters the most. Life, in its startling, vivid hues.

Your Rainbow

Let's conjure up a lovelier, brighter rainbow
    Made of jewels, translucent and opaque —
        They are you, head to toe, a rainbow "you"
            Of strength and insight, presence, and delight
              You are a rainbow of endless Light
                  You are a fountain of boundless Love
                  You are a red ruby of life
                    You are a pure amber of creation
                    You are a new gold of strength
                      You are a green emerald of affection
                    You are a blue sapphire of truth
                    You are a clear amethyst of perception
                  You are a white diamond of light
                  You are a bright diamond of light
                The jewel rainbow of your body
              The jewel rainbow of your mind
            Grounded in the solid earth
            Reaching for the lightest sky
          Dancing among distant stars
        You are Love, always Love —
You are Light with me

Imagine, A Poem of Light

Are you an apple? Or maybe
a ripe seed inside an apple of light?
You are snug and safe in the core of a torus
of light rays. You are wrapped in white
silk of light, rays emanate from your crown
to merge back into your toes, surrounding you
with a cocoon of magnetic lines. Six-winged
angels stand on all sides, protecting you.
Are you, perhaps, a fountain?
Your heart—the spring of goodness.
Liquid light overflows all over you.
Your heartbeat marks the smooth rhythm
of the gentle pulse of your crystal fountain.
The light! This miracle of light you forget about
every day as your blood carries your
heart light into every cell of your body.
Not a fountain? A star maybe?
Or two stars? A larger, iridescent one shines
on your chest—its rays so straight and dazzling.
Multicolored sparkles dance in the brightness
of your aurora. Another star on your forehead,
as brilliant and new and radiant as the heart star.
Here you are, with twin stars of light
still shining, shining, shining—

A Declaration

I am a sovereign citizen of the galaxy.
My heart goes out to the mountains.
My feet grow roots in the light.
My eyes touch the firmament of stars.
I breathe the gold air of goodness.
I drink the lucid water of joy.
Nourished by divine affection, I thrive,
linked to all living beings —
snow crystals, seeds, trees and sunlight.
In harmony, we sing the chorale of dawn.
I choose to love all, live in love.

I thank light for its warm brightness.
I thank trees for their fruit, leaves
giving oxygen, strength, and patience.
I thank water for its lucid beauty
in streams, rivers, lakes, and oceans

sustaining me, a droplet of stardust.
I thank air for flowing in my lungs
and whispering in the treetops.
I thank the universe and the stars
that exploded eons ago
for the gift of my body.
I am grateful to you all.

I am a sovereign citizen of the galaxy.
My life is a song of gratitude.
I sing, I love, I sing.

Arbor Cosmica

~ for my children

No fear, no hate, not even a mild dislike* —
we leave our heavy burdens, shards of memories
broken, all too broken, at the bottom of crystal stairs
beneath clouds of white camellias, petals swirling
through air like the snow of forgetfulness

Perfect symmetry of blossoms
points the way — up, up, always up
rainbow crystalline stairs, revealed
one by one as we ascend — inwards,
outwards — dancing spirals of our DNA

We get to know this place — these depths,
these heights — for once, for all lifetimes

With each step, pure notes resonate
and expand into clear, spacious chords —
the music of the spheres rings out, wave by wave
expanding from our open hearts

Each chord — harmonious, different —
each melody in this vast symphony
sweetly twines around another, and another
until all are One Song, One Wisdom —
of stem and flower, of leaf and root
in this Cosmic Tree of humanity

Arbor Cosmica —

We have been here
all along without knowing

Hymn of Light

> ~ *to a melody by Jean Sibelius*

Bright Sun above, its radiance all around me.
Bright Sun within, awakened by its touch.
    I breathe the Light. My heart sings of its brilliance.
    My mind, my body dance in endless Light.
        My days are full of peace, pure radiant beauty.
        Bright Sun above, my Joy, my Love, my Light.

This is my World, I'm grateful for its treasures.
This is my World, I'm thankful for its charms.
    With Joy and Peace, I praise its pure perfection.
    Earth, Water, Spirit, Fire, and Air so fine!
        My World is full of wisdom, gifts and blessings.
        My World is clear, I live in Love and Light.

This is my World, so full of grace and glory.
This is my Life, I live to love and serve.
    This is my Home, rose garden, bright and sunny.
    This is my World, my shelter of delight.
        My World is full of wisdom, gifts and blessings.
        My World is clear, I live in Love and Light.

HYMN OF LIGHT

Music by Jean Sibelius, Words by Maja Trochimczyk

Bright Sun above, its radiance all around me;

Bright Sun within, awakened by its touch;

I breathe the Light, my heart sings of its brilliance.

My mind, my body dance in endless Light.

My days are full of peace, pure radiant beauty.

Bright Sun above, my Joy, my Love, my Light.

CODA – RECIPES FOR POEMS

Spring – Mazurkas for Easter

Mazurek Królewski – The Royal Mazurka

Proportions are from *biszkopt* (sponge cake): 8 eggs+8 spoons of flour+8 spoons of sugar. Here, the flour is mostly replaced with chopped *bakalie* (nuts and dried fruit): walnuts, hazelnuts, almonds, figs, dates, raisins, plus candied orange peel, dried prunes, cranberries, and cinnamon. All mixed together with a spoonful of four so they do not form one huge clump. Chop *bakalie* and set aside. Spread some butter in the round baking pan. Preheat the oven to 350F. Separate eggs, add six spoons of sugar to egg whites, beat until stiff. Add two spoons of sugar to egg yolks, beat until whitish. Fold quickly into egg whites with one spoon of flour or ground almonds. Add the chopped *bakalie* to egg mixture, stir, pour into the pan. Bake at 350F at first, then 320F for up to 40 min. until golden brown. It will smell done! Leave to rest in the pan after taking out from the oven.

Mazurek Czekoladowy – The Chocolate Mazurka

The shortbread base is made from two cups of flour, ½ to ¾ cup of sugar, one cold whole sweet butter, chopped into the sugar+flour mixture. Mix together with three boiled egg yolks (run through a sieve), one whole egg, two or three spoons of sour cream or half-and-half, & some vanilla. Knead, form into a ball, chill in the fridge. You may replace one cup of flour with ground walnuts or almonds. After 20-30 min. spread thinly in the buttered baking pan, leaving aside some dough for decoration, bake for 30-35 min at 350F until light golden. Make the chocolate filling with ¼ pound of butter (small rectangle), one bitter chocolate bar, one milk chocolate bar, four spoons of hot half-and-half or fresh orange juice, & vanilla. Melt it all together in a pot inside a pot with boiling water, or on a non-stick pan. Spread onto the cake when cool after  baking, decorate with candied orange peel, almonds, or walnuts, as your wish. The chocolate filling could also have some sugar, cocoa and milk (3 spoons each) to make it softer & sweeter.

Summer – Pickled Pears and Plums

Pickled pears and plums include cinnamon sticks and whole cloves for flavor. To make 4 jars of pears, take 4 pounds of hard, still unripe pears, peeled and quartered. Simmer together 2/3 – 3/4 cup of 10% vinegar with 4 cups of water, ¾ cup of sugar, several sticks of cinnamon and a teaspoon of whole cloves. After peeling and coring pears, cook them in the liquid for 5 to 15 min.; they must be still hard but somewhat translucent. Place in sterilized jars, cover with liquid and seal. For four jars of pickled plums take four pounds of Italian plums (*węgierka*) , halve them and cook in one cup of 10% vinegar and 1 cup of water with ¾ cup of sugar, a teaspoon of cloves, and a cinnamon stick. Use as a side dish with meat *pasztet* that is half and half veal and pork, cooked and ground with cooked veggies (carrots, celery and parsley roots, onions), baked with eggs and breadcrumbs, nutmeg and ginger for flavor.

Babie Lato – Szarlotka

The base of half-shortbread (*ciasto pół-kruche*) is made from two cups of flour, 2/3 cup of sugar, 2/3 – 1 teaspoon of baking powder, one spoon of cinnamon, one cold whole sweet butter, chopped into the sugar+flour mixure. Mix together with three whole eggs, add 1-2 spoons of cream, if the dough is too dry. Knead, form into a ball, chill in the fridge. Meanwhile, peel and grate at least six apples – Granny Smith, Golden, or McIntosh are the best substitutes for the original Antonówka, so flavorful after baking. Mix grated apples with cinnamon, drink juice from the bottom of the bowl, so the cake is not too wet. You may add one or two grated pears for a more delicate flavor. Once apples are ready, heat the stove to 350F, spread the dough thinly in the buttered baking pan, making some "walls" around to keep the apples in. Add the apples with cinnamon, make your decorations, bake for 45 min to one hour, first at 350F then 320F, until golden brown. Check with a stick, if ready (it should come out without any dough sticking to it). Leave the cake to rest after taking out from the oven. Serve with vanilla ice-cream and a cup of hot, black tea.

Autumn – Bigos and Salads

Bigos or Hunter's Stew

This dish improves when frozen and reheated, as it used to be made for winter hunting trips to be warmed up by bonfire. The stew consists of equal amounts of washed sauerkraut and fresh sliced cabbage, plus pork and beef. Start from two chopped onions that are simmered in oil until translucent. Add the two cabbages for 30 minutes (drain & rinse the sauerkraut, if too sour). Simmer in an uncovered pot, so the cabbage stink evaporates; add water if needed. Separately, brown cubes of good pork and beef cuts (pork-loin or shoulder), add to the cabbage with spices – min. 10 seeds each of peppercorn, allspice, juniper, no more than 5 bay leaves, and salt to taste. Add five dried mushrooms (*prawdziwek*, Boletus) that were soaked in water to remove sand and sliced. After about two hours, add some slices from a smoked Polish sausage (not essential, since most have a fake smoked scent). For the last 30 minutes add up to 10 prunes and two handfuls of black raisins. Never use tomatoes, chili, or paprika; these are not Polish spices and will ruin the flavor. Stir frequently while cooking to make sure it does not burn. If you made too much, freeze portions in containers. Serve with potatoes, or pumpernickel, or rye bread without caraway seeds, these are the wrong flavor, do not belong with bigos.

Celery Salad

Peel and grate one whole celery root, grate one or two peeled apples, such as Granny Smith, McIntosh, or Gala. Squeeze some lemon juice to keep color intact. Mix with mayonnaise and sour cream (half and half each), add some golden raisins or dried cranberries. Enjoy fresh; this salad does not keep due to the presence of the cream and mayonnaise.

Potato Salad

Cook and chop into cubes or small slices two pounds of potatoes, some carrots, celery root,& parsley root. For more flavor, peel after cooking not before. Add one cup of cooked sweet peas, at least four chopped pickles, & two chopped boiled eggs. Mix with mayonnaise, add some pickle juice, if it tastes too bland. Add salt and pepper to taste. Refrigerate, to serve with cold cuts and fresh sourdough bread.

Winter – Barszcz, Kompot, and Kutia

Barszcz Wigilijny

To serve at Wigilia, Christmas Eve dinner, make proper Polish *barszcz*. Peel at least two pounds of beets, one onion, some celery root, carrots, and parsnips. Chop into pieces, add peppercorn, allspice and bay leaves (more pepper than the rest), and two dried whole mushrooms. After bringing to boil, add two spoons of vinegar to preserve color. Cook on low heat until vegetables are soft and can be poked with a fork. Throw out all veggies except beets. Serve with chopped beets from the soup and *uszka,* small pierogi stuffed with a wild mushroom filling. Since I do not know how to make them, you are on your own. You may also serve this *barszcz* to drink in teacups, with wild-mushroom-filled pastry or blintzes (*krokiety z grzybami*). In contrast, Ukrainian *barszcz* has more veggies, all chopped together, including both beets and cabbage, never found in the elegant Polish *barszcz*.

Kompot Wigilijny

This is my favorite flavor of Christmas, but few people like it. Cook in big pot of water a mixture of dried apples, pears, figs, dates, raisins, apricots, with some prunes, cinnamon sticks and just a couple of cloves. Add a spoon of honey if not sweet enough. Serve with fruit in bowls or in cups to drink.. I like taking the fruit, draining it, chopping and using as a filling for *szarlotka* base, adding some ground nuts.

Kutia

This dessert for Wigilia is from eastern Borderlands of Poland. Cook in milk one pound of poppy seeds, cool, grind three times in a meat grinder; wash before cooking to remove sand. Set aside. Chop dates, figs, raisins, candied orange peel, some prunes, as well as lots of walnuts, almonds, and hazelnuts. Key flavors are dates, figs and walnuts. Mix into the ground poppy seed, add honey to taste (never use any sugar, the buckwheat honey is the best). Fry with lots of butter on low heat mixing frequently. You may add some cinnamon and vanilla for flavor. Put into a bowl and refrigerate, decorating with whole peeled almonds and/or walnut halves. Serve with shortbread cookies made like the mazurka base, cut into stars. You can eat one spoon at a time, not more. This very rich dessert may also be used as filling for *makowiec,* a poppy seed roll made with yeast dough.

L: At Scenic Drive Gallery, Monrovia, CA, 2013. R: a 4-year-old Maja in her garden at Jelonki, a suburb of Warsaw, 1962. Photo by Henryka Trochimczyk.

Marcin, Ian, Ania, Mom in Santa Monica, 2011.

About the Author

Maja Trochimczyk with Grandson Adam Depinski, Thanksgiving 2019.

Maja Trochimczyk, PhD, is a Polish American poet, music historian, photographer, and non-profit director. She is the author/editor of eight books on music and Polish culture in Polish and English, as well as five poetry volumes and four anthologies, most recently *We Are Here: Village Poets Anthology* (co-edited with Marlene Hitt, 2020). A former Poet Laureate of Sunland-Tujunga, she is the founder of Moonrise Press, President of the California State Poetry Society, Managing Editor of the *California Quarterly* and *Poetry Letter* published by the CSPS, and President of the Helena Modjeska Art and Culture Club, promoting Polish culture in California. Hundreds of her poems, articles and book chapters appeared in English, Polish, and in a variety of translations. She presented her research at over 90 international conferences and received many awards from Polish, Canadian and American institutions. Among other honors, she is the winner of the Creative Arts Prize from the Polish American Historical Association (2016) for her two books about Polish civilian experience during WW II and its aftermath, Slicing the Bread and The Rainy Bread. Since 2010, she has maintained a series of blogs on poetry, Polish history and culture, with a total readership of over 970,000 visitors: moonrisepress.com; californiastatepoetrysociety.com; poetrylaurels.blogspot.com; chopinwithcherries.blogspot.com, etc.

www.ingramcontent.com/pod-product-compliance
Lightning Source LLC
Chambersburg PA
CBHW042128010526
44111CB00030B/18